GOD OF THE IMPOSSIBLE

30-Prayers for the Redemption and Restoration of California

KATHY J. CHASTAIN

GOD OF THE IMPOSSIBLE!: 30-DAYS OF PRAYER
Copyright © 2024
by Kathy J. Chastain

ISBN-13: 979-8-9914962-0-9

Published by
Last Arrow Ministries, Inc.
246 W Caldwell Ave
Visalia CA 93277
Email: info@lastarrow.org

Table of Contents

Dedication

This book is dedicated to all who love and pray for California and our Nation. May we endeavor to become One Nation Under God, once again.

To my Lord, my friend and the lover of my soul, Jesus.
It is through Him, that I live, and move, and have my being. (Acts 17:28 KJV)

Acknowledgements

I dreamt of becoming an author for the first time in 1996 while I was in a time of prayer. On that fateful day, I felt impressed by the Lord to write a certain book with a certain title. I had been a backslider for several years and was learning things for the first time as a newly rededicated Christian. I was naïve to the timing of the Lord and began to outline that particular book. That book has not been written yet, and now that I understand more about the ways in which God works in my life, I have come to believe that may possibly be the last book I write.

Since 1996, I have started and outlined numerous books, all yet to be written.

In 2022, I wrote my very first book with the help of my friend and colleague, Christopher Dalton. That book, "Redeem California, With God All Things Are Possible" also came from the prompting and inspiration of the Lord. I felt it was an urgent word and needed to get out as soon as possible.

Chris has been a constant part of my life since my official writing journey began. He has been the instrument God used to help bring into fruition what the Lord placed upon my heart. He and his wife, Carissa, have been supportive and patient with me throughout the many emails, questions and changes along the way. I am so grateful for his knowledge and help as I learn and grow. Thank you, Chris, for all you have done to make these books possible!

To Amanda Lang, my second editor, who has been a friend for many many years. When I was in the fitness industry, she was a client. When I opened a runaway homeless youth shelter for girls, she showed up to help, no questions asked, just said "what can I do?" When I make spelling errors in my social media posts, she graciously sends me a text to show my error so that I do not look unprofessional. She has always been there to help in so many ways, because that is who she is. She is a true friend. Beyond that, we have somewhat different political and theological beliefs. Amanda never, ever judges me or allows our differences to divide us. She gives me feedback on subject matters and easily presents the other side in grace and kindness. I really appreciate that, and I am grateful our differences haven't come between our friendship. The prayers and the content of this book are both political and theological in nature, so when she volunteered to edit the final version of this book, it meant a great deal to me. Thank you so much Amanda for your friendship over the many years and for your honesty along the way! You are my spelling and grammar guru. Thank you for your help in making me look better then what I could have done on my own. You are a cherished friend!

To my friends, Regan and Tanya Sunderland, pastors of Tulare Bethel Church, Tulare, California. Regan and Tanya have been a consistent source of support through friendship, prayer and monthly contributions to the mission of Redeem California. Regan was one of the first people, if not the first person, I spoke with when I felt the prompting of the Lord to pursue the mission of Redeem California. He is a pastor who doesn't shy away from the hard topics affecting the church in today's culture. I appreciate him so much. When the church adopted Redeem California as an urban missionary and chose to contribute monthly to the organization, it was an answer to prayer. Their support has helped me continue in spreading the message of faith, that God can and will do the impossible in California. Thank you, Regan and Tanya for believing with me!

To my pastor and cousin, Jeremy Cain, Pentecostal Lighthouse, Visalia CA., Thank you for your unwavering encouragement, prayer and counsel. Many times, over the past couple of years, I have wondered if I missed God; questioning the mission of Redeem California, wondering if my last book and this book was my own ambition or if I was being obedient to what I felt the Lord whisper. Every time, my pastor waded through the confusion I was experiencing. He encouraged me and reminded me that I would never go wrong stepping out in faith, knowing that God doesn't waste anything we do for him.

I am so grateful for my pastor's life, the way he leads and the grace he allows me as I grow in my walk with the Lord. He is kind, compassionate and unwavering in Biblical truth. Thank you for never compromising and for gently and kindly providing counsel and truth at times when I was struggling to see the end in sight. I am forever grateful for you!

Lastly, to my family and friends who have loved me, encouraged me and believed in me. You will never know how much it has meant, but I hope over time, I will be able to show you my gratitude and love. Thank you for loving me!

Introduction

Every year at years end, I spend the day alone, reflecting on all that has transpired throughout the year. I read through my journal and the prayers I have written, careful to be aware of the ones that have been answered, and thoughtful of things yet to be fulfilled or understood. I spend time in prayer listening for what God might say or impress upon me for the upcoming year. I think about new goals I'd like to work toward as the year transitions.

On December 31, 2018, I was doing just that. I had spent most of the day alone and had decided to go to my church to pray. There are times I like to go to the church and pray instead of praying at home, there is just something different I feel when I am able to that. So as I got to the church, I was surprised to notice that I didn't feel to stop, but instead, I felt to drive past the church and out to the county Juvenal Detention Facility to pray there. I didn't know why, I had never done that before, but this day that is what I felt to do.

When I arrived, I pulled over on the side of the road with a perfect view of the facility and I began to pray. I don't recall what I prayed but I do know exactly what happened when I opened my mouth and began to pray.

I had an open vision.

As I was looking at the Juvenal Detention Center, I could see thousands of black birds swirling around the building. There were so

many, it looked like a swirling black whirlwind, but I could clearly see
they were black birds, thousands of them. But when I opened my mouth
to pray, all of a sudden, the whirlwind of birds immediately left the
building and descended upon my car. They had heard my voice praying
and they came to where I was. I instinctively felt the birds represented
evil and I had an audience with them because I was praying. I wasn't
afraid, I was just aware. As I prayed, and the stronger my prayer got, I
suddenly saw a huge beam of light coming out of heaven like a laser and
penetrating the center of the facility. It was a powerful experience and an
incredible sight to see.

That experience caused me to understand what happens in the spirit
realm when we speak and just how powerful our prayers are. I had always
been taught that prayer changes things, and that prayer was powerful,
but until that moment, I only understood it intellectually and through
belief, but that experience gave me revelation knowledge.

Then I remembered a passage of scripture I had read long ago. I
quickly went to my Bible app to search it out. The verse is Ecclesiastes
10:20 "Do not curse the king, even in your thought; and do not curse
the rich, even in thy bedroom; FOR A BIRD OF THE AIR MAY CARRY YOUR
VOICE, AND A BIRD IN FLIGHT MAY TELL THE MATTER." Wow! God was
showing me how important our voice is!

The Bible tells us that "death and life is in the power of the tongue."
(Proverbs 18:21 NKJV). Prayer is a combination of words, spoken to
God that has the power! Prayer is literally creating life in situations, and
in people when directed to God Almighty. It is something to consider.
Similarly, we can also speak death when we speak condemnation,
judgement and negativity. I wonder if the evil spirits that represented as
birds in my vision was attracted to the words spoken by all the inmates
in the detention facility and they had to leave when I began to pray, not
only did they leave, but the light of God replaced it.

GOD OF THE IMPOSSIBLE!

Since that time, I have understood the power of prayer and the power of the spoken word. When the Bible says that, "one can put a thousand to flight and two can put ten thousand to flight" (Duet 32:30 NKJV) what could happen if 10, 50, or thousands of us began to pray in unity, collectively praying the prayers written in the pages of this book?

When I wrote out these prayers, they were written for pastors to lead their congregations in what I had hoped would be 30 days of prayer for our state leading up to the elections. However, I have come to realize, and I am sure many of you have also realized, some pastors and ministers of the Bible do not talk about the condition of our communities, schools or the political landscape that is literally abolishing our history and removing God from everything, destroying our constitution in the process. I don't understand that, but I know that God does.

In the pages that follow, you will find 30 prayers, 30 declarations to go with each prayer, and 30 short essays I wrote for each prayer. I wrote these prayers for seven specific categories targeting the area's I felt most needed in this hour. Some of the prayers are strong in our request of the Lord, and they are all biblical. The categories of prayer are:

- Repentance
- Forgiveness
- Government
- Families
- Schools
- Children
- Law Enforcement

You can use this book as a daily devotional or a 30-week devotional. If you chose the 30-week approach, I suggest you read the passage on the first day and pray the prayer daily for seven days in a row, and then move on to the next chapter. I believe if you chose to speak these prayers and declarations once, or seven days in a row, God will still hear and answer.

May you be blessed and be encouraged with the knowledge that we serve the God of the IMPOSSIBLE!

"The size of your prayers
reveal the perception you have
of the size of your God,"

- Eli Lopez

Chapter One
God of the Impossible

As we start praying over our cities, state, and nation, you will notice that when I begin my prayers, I begin with "Lord." That is just my way of addressing God in these written prayers. I recognize that everyone prays differently, so I hope my language choice doesn't trip anyone up.

I am sure many of us have differing theology and denominational backgrounds. That should not divide us if we are all reading the same Bible and endeavoring to make it to Heaven. Accepting differences, just like in a marriage, leads to unity, which we desperately need at this hour. The Lord's job is to lead us into all truth through the unity of faith (Eph 4:13).

You will notice that all scripture references are from the King James Version. I grew up reading that translation, and that is what I know. Please feel free to use whatever translation you feel most comfortable with.

I also want to stress the importance of saying these prayers verbally instead of silently. All throughout scripture, words were spoken with voice. That sentence might sound redundant, but many people pray in their minds and do not vocalize their prayers. I do that myself at times and meditate on God's word. But for the purposes of these prayers, I hope you will say each word out loud and speak them into the atmosphere.

To give an example of how powerful a word spoken into the atmosphere can be, look at what the Bible says in Ecclesiastes 10:20:

"Curse not the king, not in thy thought; and curse not the rich in thy bedchamber; for a bird of the air shall carry the voice, and that which hath wings shall tell the matter."

We must not only be careful of what we say but also be purposeful in what we pray. With that, let's begin!

Each prayer is to be prayed as the collective body of Christ (we), and the first prayer is taken from Philippians 4:13: "I can do all things through him who strengthens me."

We know that God does not fail. Failure comes through us; from fear, from unbelief, from weariness, from forgetfulness, and from laziness. We need the strength of the Lord in this hour for various areas of our lives; this has to be more than just words. We must look at ourselves and ask God to reveal the areas in each of us where fear, unbelief, weariness, forgetfulness, and laziness play a role in our prayer life and walk with God.

Our adversary is the master deceiver, and he is excellent at masking things in our life and calling it something other than what it is. Fear can often be masked by a false state of silence. We think we are wise in not speaking about a topic when it is really fear of what someone will think of us.

I am guilty of this, especially when I post on social media. I have deleted countless posts for fear that someone would misunderstand my meaning. I am working on this however, and becoming braver with speaking up when I feel it is important. Truth should be non-negotiable, and we can speak the truth in love, and the truth will do its job to set people free.

Unbelief is a slippery slope. It is an especially important topic regarding the prayers we pray.

Do we really believe God will Redeem California, or are we just going through the motions of the prayer?

Do we really believe God will heal the sick?

It is easy to let unbelief creep in when often our prayers are delayed, and circumstances look bleak. Belief and unbelief are heart positions. If we know that God is good, that He desires to Redeem California and to heal the sick, the issues don't lie with whether we are worthy for God to answer our prayers, but they rest on the truth of His word and what He has promised. We must know that God can and will perform His word. Instead of having unbelief, we must ask Him to reveal what hinders the prayers from being answered. More on that in the coming chapters.

Weariness, forgetfulness, and laziness are also increasing among us all. We have far more stress, debt, responsibilities, and distractions than at any other time in history.

Now more than ever, we must redeem the time.

We must carefully and purposefully choose how we spend our time, making time to be a vessel for the Lord to use, especially with our prayers.

So as you think about the words to this prayer and as you pray it daily in this chapter, think about the areas in your life where you need strength, that you will be able to do "all things" that He is calling you to do, with Him who gives you strength.

DAY 1

Lord, you said in your word, I can do all things through Christ who strengthens me, we pray for strength to declare your word in this hour and strength to stand for righteousness in our City, State and Nation.

Declaration

We declare that Christians will rise up across our cities, states and nations and stand for righteousness and truth in Jesus name.

GOD OF THE IMPOSSIBLE!

KATHY J· CHASTAIN

Chapter Two
The Sovereignty of God

Do you ever think about the sovereignty of God? I suppose if we were British, we might understand that concept a bit better since the UK has a King. None of us really understand how big God is in his sovereignty because we don't relate to him as a King.

The word sovereign means "possessing supreme or ultimate power."

The Bible tells us that all nations, governments, and rulers lie in God's hands. Scripture shows us that Jesus has defeated all the principalities and powers in the heavenly places. The ruling spiritual forces, who work through human authorities, are subject to Jesus, King of Kings and Lord of Lords. (Rev 17:14 KJV).

Jesus is King over all things.

This isn't easy to grasp when it looks exactly the opposite of God being in control. It's hard to watch the state of California impose unconstitutional laws and see Jesus as the King of California. It's difficult to reconcile what we see taking place in our schools and to our children and hold tight to the belief God is in control.

So, if Jesus is Lord of all, and the Government is under His control, why is all this craziness taking place?

Despite the difficulty of maintaining faith in the face of great obstacles, God requires His children to partner with Him using the authority he gave us when we took on his name in baptism. The name Jesus. When we died to our old nature, we were created as a new creation in Him; we now "live and move and have our being in him" (Acts 17:28 KJV). This is how he set it up from the beginning. In the Garden, God created man and woman to be His ambassadors, made in His image, put here to rule and reign with Him. We have failed in that often because we don't quite understand who we are in him.

So, in our failure, and in the Bible when the children of Israel failed, He has been known to move all by Himself without the help of humanity. That is what we are asking him to do now in this prayer.

Part of that ruling and reigning is done through our prayers. I know many Americans are praying for our nation, and many are praying for California. We are where we are for numerous reasons, none of which I will address today. But suffice it to say, it is time we ask God to forgive us for our indifference along the way, and ask him to move in a powerful way to change California and our country.

We are to pray for all leaders, good and bad, Christian and non-Christian (see 1 Timothy 2:1-4).

We are to pray for ungodly leaders to be removed and godly leaders to be lifted and put into place. This is what today's prayer is focused on. We want to see God's sovereign hand work in miraculous ways to remove and replace leaders in power.

Throughout history and scripture God works in and through difficult times, and in and through difficult, even evil, people (read Daniel 2-3). God is in control at all times and in all places, and He wants us to step up and help Him through prayer and more.

God is at work and holds all of time in His hands. When we are aligned with His will, our prayers impact the rulers of California. They work with the all-powerful, all-controlling God to ensure that His plans and ideas will be done on earth as they are in Heaven.

DAY 2

Lord, we ask that you would Sovereignly remove wicked leaders who stand against your word, and replace them with the right people who will restore righteous values to the people in California.

Declaration

We thank you Lord, for exposing the wicked leaders in our state and nation and we declare new leaders are rising even now who will restore righteous values in the state of California. In Jesus name.

Chapter Three
The Return of The Fear of the Lord

I grew up in a holy roller Pentecostal church–the kind of church where people ran the aisles, the preacher climbed over pews while preaching, and saints expected the manifest presence of God to show up in every service. I grew up knowing, from experience, that God was real, Heaven was real, Hell was real, and the Devil was most certainly real. It was a time when society made fun of the Pentecostal church and other denominations said things like "all that Pentecostals preach is hell, fire, and brimstone."

That was not too far from the truth. There was an emphasis on the reality of eternity and the need for a savior. I had a healthy fear of the Lord, as many did 40 years ago. California was amid the "Jesus Revolution," and revival was spreading. The first Left Behind movie came out when I was about 11 years old. I am not sure if it was called "Left Behind," but the movie was about the rapture of the saints and how the world would respond when, suddenly, people witnessed others caught up in the heavens. I will never forget it. Our youth group watched it, and I decided that I did not want to be left behind that night.

Over time, the messages about eternity began to fade, and the church no longer reached for the lost; instead, it became a combination of many other things. When this happened, we became irrelevant to the world –

possibly irrelevant to the Lord. We became complacent, not on purpose but probably out of ignorance.

Growing up, I had such a close relationship with the Lord. I felt like he was my friend. I talked to him about everything, and I felt safest and most loved when I was in his presence. As I aged, I did not know how to live in this world and the world that existed with me and Jesus. They seemed incompatible, and my young heart and mind didn't know how to reconcile the two dichotomies. I desperately wanted to abide in Him and never leave that place of being in his presence. But alas, I had to live in this world, and it turns out I was about to take the wrong turn in life.

Through all the many mistakes I made in my history, I never meant to leave the Lord. I always loved and wanted more of him, but I ignorantly took him for granted. I saw him as my friend. I failed to see him as the Almighty, who sits on the circle of time, with the earth as his footstool. I did not know him that way. I didn't know how important obedience was; I just trusted that he knew my heart. That was until a fateful night in May 2010.

I was, I thought, living for God. I was going to church, praying, reading my Bible, trying to make a very difficult marriage work, and trying not to run, which was my default in times past. The fact that I wasn't running proved that God was working in my life. We were separated, and I was staying with a friend after being kicked out of my home for the 4th or 15th time (there were too many to count). The Lord had been dealing with me about something he was asking of me. I had been negotiating with him for months in my thoughts, justifying what I was not ready to release to Him. I thought I was "ok" with Him; I had no idea I wasn't.

That night, I went to bed as usual, and then at midnight, I was awakened from a dead sleep by what I believe was the angel of the Lord. I sat straight up in bed wide awake, trembling in fear, because I felt that the angel had come for my soul that night. I had an awareness that my time was up, and I was not ready to meet Jesus. I tried to pray, I tried to repent, but the tears would not come, I could not find a place of repentance. I was not ready and terrified that it was too late. Although I could not feel anything other than a calm stillness, I said to the Lord, I will do whatever you ask of me; I will be whatever you want me to be if you will give me another chance, and the time to make it right. God had mercy on me that night, as I am still here to tell you about that experience. I was forever changed that night, and I began to understand that God cares about a lot of things that I had never realized before. I knew there was one thing in particular he was asking of me, and I complied willingly.

That night, I saw a different side of God and understood, for the first time, what the fear of the Lord was. The fear of the Lord is not fear, as we know fear. It was the Lord in his majesty and power, his dominion and justice, his Almightiness; it was reverence. Words do not adequately describe the revelation I received that night. I am forever thankful God had mercy on me and revealed a new side of Himself that I had never known before. That was the beginning of when I learned that God wanted a reciprocal relationship with me. I learned that if I loved Him as I professed I did, my love should show through obedience to his word. "If you love me, keep my commandments" had a whole new meaning for me. (John 14:15 NKJV).

The church as a whole has lost the Fear of the Lord, not because they meant to, but because life has become busy and cumbersome, with many distractions and things that entertain us. It is easy to coast on autopilot when people, places, and things run our lives instead of God.

We need a reality check, a shaking to wake us up to the reality of eternity. The Fear of the Lord is a mercy gift to those who need to get their lives right with God. It is a Mercy gift to California and the United States to remember who is in control. The Fear of the Lord is desperately needed in this hour to turn our nation back to God, the same God this country was founded on.

The Bible says, "The Fear of the Lord is the beginning of wisdom" (Proverbs 9:10). I believe much will change if we begin to pray for a fresh revelation of the Fear of the Lord to fall on California and the United States. I believe then people will begin to understand just how far we have strayed, and how desperately we need to repent as a nation.

Please pray this prayer with me.

DAY 3

*Lord, we ask that you would cause
the Fear of the Lord to fall on
California & America and we ask that
you would revive and redeem the hearts
of people throughout our state
and across our country.
In Jesus name we pray! Let it be
so according to your will!*

Declaration

Lord, we declare that the fear of the Lord will revive hearts and redeem people throughout California and our nation. In Jesus name.

Chapter Four
Surrendered in Grief

Recently, a sad reality has come to light for many friends and family members: life is unpredictable. Two families in Redding, California, lost their sons in a landslide while camping. These precious boys and their families are dear friends of my son's family. They are in community together. The mothers are in a weekly bible study with my daughter-inlaw.

One of the boys attended school with my granddaughter, and they were on the same school sports team.The day after the tragedy, I laid next to my 10-year-old granddaughter as she cried herself to sleep. She continued to cry herself to sleep for several nights as I write this chapter. She has known these boys since infancy, and she is now at an age to understand the deep sadness death brings into our lives.

Yet, amid their grief, I sat with my son and daughter-in-law as they put on worship music, held their daughter, prayed together, and cried together as a family.

I wept in thankfulness as I listened to my daughter-in-law say, "In all this, Lord, we know that you are still good."

In that moment of great pain and sorrow, peace flooded me as a parent when I witnessed their turning to Jesus for strength and comfort and modeling that dependency on Jesus for my granddaughter.

When death comes into our life, we cannot help but reflect on our own future. Even though all of us endeavor to serve the Lord daily with our lives, death is an ever-present reality that humbles all of us.

As I reflect on this tremendous loss that will affect countless people in the Redding community, I understand that there will be many questions for God that may never have answers on this side of heaven. Heartbreak such as this leaves a wound in our soul that only Jesus can heal. It also simultaneously creates an opportunity for the enemy to accuse God or accuse others.

None of us have gotten to where we are in life without pain and heartbreak. I have observed that pain is often looking for someone or something to blame. When there is nothing to blame, we can easily fall into despair.

The heart must find a way to continue to live, and in doing so, we form our own conclusions and come up with our own answers to the unanswerable questions. These become the "stories we tell ourselves," as Brené Brown would say.

This is the place where fear, unbelief, bitterness, and all sorts of other hidden beliefs can take root without our awareness and sometimes without our permission, due mostly to the brutal pain of life. This brings me to this chapter's prayer, which is on forgiveness.

In my personal prayer life, I start all my prayers asking for forgiveness, especially for unintentional sins or words spoken that inadvertently could have caused hurt to someone. I am a mental health therapist, and there are opportunities for me to miss the hurt in therapy. When counseling couples I am often in a position to tell hard truths that can hurt, so I always clear the slate with God when I pray.

I also think it is good for us to humble ourselves in surrender to Him when we go to Him in prayer.

GOD OF THE IMPOSSIBLE!

This chapter, our prayer is, "...Lord, forgive me. Reveal to me the hidden things in my heart and cleanse me completely, that I may be a vessel of honor for you."

There have been times in prayer when the Lord has brought a memory to my mind that I had forgotten all about. One day in prayer years ago, a particular memory of my son surfaced. This memory, during his baby years, was a good memory and, at the same time, one that caused me deep sorrow.

I wept and wept as the Lord reminded me of that memory. I had forgotten all about it, but I heard the Lord speak to my heart and say, "you forgot but I did not forget."

I suddenly realized how many things get buried deep down in the human heart, but God sees them all.

Since then, I have prayed that God would reveal any hidden things in my heart.

Working with patients, I have also seen first-hand how fragmented the heart can be. When we give God permission to shine his light into every area of our heart and forgive us for things we have forgotten about or disregarded, not only does it bring forgiveness, but it also brings deep healing in unimaginable ways.

Today and this week, pray and meditate on this prayer with me. Let us all become clean vessels of honor that God can and will flow through.

DAY 4

*Lord, as we begin to pray for
our families, communities,
and our state, we first
ask for forgiveness.
Lord forgive me,
reveal to me the the hidden things
in my heart and cleanse
me completely that I may be
a vessel of honor for you
In Jesus name!*

Declaration

We thank you Lord for your forgiveness and we know that you will continue to reveal the hidden things in our heart. We declare that we will be a vessel of honor to be used by you for your purpose, and your glory in Jesus name.

GOD OF THE IMPOSSIBLE!

Chapter Five
The Evil of the World

The Bible says in James 5:17, "The effectual fervent prayer of the righteous availeth much." It is easy to pray fervent prayers when it comes to our children. Jesus said, speaking of little children, "Whoever shall offend one of these little ones who believes in me, it would be better for him to have a millstone hanged around his neck and cast into the depth of the sea." When the disciples ask Jesus who was the greatest in the kingdom, he called a little child and set the child in the midst of them and said "except ye be converted and become as little children, you shall not enter into the kingdom of heaven." (Matthew 18:1-7 KJV). It is easy to see through scripture the value the Lord places on children. As if that weren't enough, the majority of society also places great value on children. We love them and our need to protect them is visceral, largely due to their innocence and inability to protect themselves.

Children are particularly vulnerable to abuse for several reasons, including their developmental stage, dependency on adults, and social dynamics. Here are some things that make children so vulnerable:

Developmental Vulnerability

Children, especially young ones, are still developing physically, emotionally, and cognitively, making it difficult for them to understand, resist, or report abuse. Their limited knowledge and experience can make them easy targets for manipulative or coercive behaviors by abusers.

Dependency and Trust

Children rely heavily on adults for their basic needs, safety, and emotional support. This dependency can be exploited by abusers, particularly if the abuser is someone the child trusts or depends on, such as a family member, teacher, or caregiver.

Power Imbalance

The inherent power imbalance between adults and children can lead to situations where children feel powerless or too afraid to speak out against an abuser. This fear can be reinforced if the abuser uses threats or manipulation to maintain control over the child.

Lack of Awareness and Education

Children often lack the awareness and education to recognize inappropriate behavior and may not understand what constitutes abuse. Without proper (maybe 'appropriate' is a better word) education on these issues, children are less likely to identify and report abuse.

Social and Cultural Factors

Cultural norms and societal attitudes can also play a role. In some cultures, children are taught to obey authority figures without question, which can discourage them from reporting abuse. Additionally, stigma and shame associated with abuse can prevent children and their families from seeking help.

GOD OF THE IMPOSSIBLE!

The media is not short on stories of schoolteachers and coaches who have been caught sexually abusing one of their students. Predators target sensitive kids, disenfranchised kids, and those children who struggle socially. They are wickedly good at singling out vulnerable children.

Sexual abuse is not the only abuse taking place in schools. I have heard numerous stories of teachers and coaches who belittle, bully, and intimidate students, leaving them feeling humiliated, worthless, and afraid.

Children are the number one target of the devil, making them the number one target of those with perverse, sadistic and evil appetites. They are the future generation; to break them, to defile them, to traumatize them, creates a generation that is easy to manipulate, control and make dependent on Big Brother, because they growup in a weakened physical and emotional state, with an intellectual deficit. Research is replete with data that proves this premise. Additionally, the ACES (Adverse Childhood Experiences Scale), which is a questionnaire developed in the 1990s by the Centers for Disease Control and Prevention (CDC) and Kaiser Permanente, measures traumatic events that occur during childhood, such as abuse, neglect, and household dysfunction. The impact of such experiences on the long-term health and well-being of a child is provable and predictable. Below is an overview of the dangers associated with a score of four or more:

Physical Health Problems

- Chronic Diseases: Higher ACE scores are linked to a greater risk of chronic diseases such as heart disease, diabetes, and obesity. Studies show that individuals with four or more ACEs are twice as likely to develop heart disease and diabetes.
- Neurological Effects: High ACEs can lead to changes in brain development, affecting areas responsible for emotional regulation,

decision-making, and stress responses. This can result in increased susceptibility to neurological disorders and cognitive impairments.

Mental Health Issues

- Depression and Anxiety: Children with high ACE scores are more likely to develop mental health disorders, including depression, anxiety, and PTSD. The risk of depressive episodes increases significantly with the number of ACEs.
- Substance Abuse: There is a strong correlation between ACEs and substance abuse. Individuals with high ACE scores are more likely to use alcohol, drugs, and tobacco as coping mechanisms.

Behavioral and Social Problems

- Aggressive and Antisocial Behavior: Children with high ACE scores are at increased risk for aggressive behavior, conduct disorders, and involvement in criminal activities. These behaviors can persist into adulthood, leading to legal and social consequences.
- Academic and Employment Challenges: ACEs can negatively impact academic performance and educational attainment, leading to difficulties in securing stable employment and achieving economic stability later in life.

Interpersonal Relationship Issues

- Attachment Problems: Traumatic childhood experiences can impair the ability to form secure attachments, resulting in difficulties forming and maintaining healthy relationships throughout life.
- Parenting Challenges: Individuals with high ACE scores may struggle with parenting, potentially perpetuating a cycle of trauma and adversity for the next generation.

Increased Risk of Violence and Victimization

- Exposure to Violence: High ACEs are associated with a greater likelihood of being involved in violent relationships, either as a victim or perpetrator. This includes domestic violence, intimate partner violence, and community violence.
- Victimization: High ACE scores increase the risk of being victimized in adulthood, including sexual and physical assault.

To ensure the safety of our children, and in an effort to protect the future of our society, we must pray for hedges of protection around our kids, whether biological or those whom we encounter in our neighborhoods, churches, social clubs and schools, and we must pray against those who wish to harm them. Kids are struggling like never before and they need our prayers.

This prayer is a plea for God to intervene and rebuke the demonic forces working through people who target our children. We are asking Him to divinely move in a way that brings change to the education system across California and the United States. We are asking Him to remove and expose people working in our schools who wish harm to our children, and to replace them with people who will cherish and protect our children, the most vulnerable of humanity.

I truly believe we are going to see great change come to California. What has been exposed in our schools has been necessary for us to understand the vast ways the enemy of our soul has infiltrated every area of society.

I know all of you reading this agree with me, but I want to encourage you today: God is fighting with us and for us! He is moving on behalf of the prayers of the saints, and we will see the tide change.

*Lord, we ask that
you would rebuke the demonic
influence in our schools.
Remove every teacher or adult
that would seek to harm our
children in any predatory way.
Expose abusers and fill our
schools with people who will
love and protect our kids
In Jesus name!*

Declaration

Lord, we declare that the demonic influences in our schools will be purged. We declare that every teacher and adult who would seek to cause harm to our children would be removed. In Jesus name.

GOD OF THE IMPOSSIBLE!

Chapter Six
Breaking Generational Curses

This topic may be controversial for some. If that is the case, I hope that you will search out the scriptures, ask questions and keep an open mind on what I am hoping to convey in the topic below.

This prayer is about asking God to break abuse cycles that run in our families. I imagine you are not willfully participating in abuse, but there is a high probability, according to research, that you have been a victim of abuse by a parent, loved one or trusted authority figure. While this chapter's prayer is specific to abuse, there may be other cycles operating in your life that you'd like to release to God. The word "cycle" is a secular term used in psychology to address patterns of behavior. The Biblical equivalent is the word stronghold, which is a pattern of beliefs that results in behaviors.

We find in the book of Exodus, Numbers, Deuteronomy, even Ezekiel, the concept of generational curses and generational blessings. Although the Old Covenant (Old Testament) has been replaced with the New Covenant (New Testament), when studying the scripture, we must study it as a whole. The entire Bible is the inspired word of God. The New Testament confirms the Old Testament; everything in the Bible fits perfectly together.

Up until 2017, generational curses were not things I had ever thought about. I knew it was part of the Old Testament, but when reading my Bible, I didn't give it a second thought. I just filed it away somewhere in my mind.

Then one fateful day in 2017, I attended the California Association of Marriage & Family Therapists Conference in San Francisco. It was my first conference, and I was excited to be there. Even though I am in the field of psychology, I am a Christian-Based Psychotherapist and have seen time and again how Psychology proves the Bible. Without knowing it, I was about to discover that generational curses in the Bible was being taught in the field of psychology.

The class I took that day was on Intergenerational Trauma, otherwise known as epigenetics. The speaker was a medical doctor, who had previously held a PhD in Psychology before having a mental breakdown. As the speaker began to describe her history of psychosis, auditory and visual hallucinations with no apparent medical reason, all I could think of while she was speaking was, she was being spiritually attacked and was able to see and hear in the spirit realm, according to the experiences she described.

However, because science gives no credence to the invisible world, where God exists, she was unable to find answers to what was ailing her. This led her on a journey of more school and research, ultimately discovering the science of epigenetics.

Epigenetics says that cells have memory, and that generational trauma can be passed down through the bloodline and affect the next generation. The speaker believed her brain malady was a result of generational trauma--epigenetics. I was in awe: once again, science was proving the Bible.

The phrase "generational curse" offends many people. None of us would raise our hand and say a curse has impacted our lives. Yet, if we think about it, most of us have been affected by a generational curse in some form or fashion. Let me explain.

GOD OF THE IMPOSSIBLE!

Science has determined that sexual abuse, physical abuse, emotional abuse, addiction, suicide, homosexuality, incest, criminal conduct, gambling, poverty, wealth, mental health issues, diseases, critical natures, anger, and so on, are generational in nature. Using sexual and physical abuse as an example, that is almost always generational. In the family unit, abuse has occurred to the parents and grandparents and it is passed down generationally. The same is true for addiction, criminality and all the other manifestations of things I mentioned above. These things are passed down and become strongholds to us and opportunities for the enemy to work in our lives.

Whether generational strongholds come through nature or nurture, we need to recognize them for what they are, so that we can break them with the power of prayer, a renewed mind, and the application of the blood of Jesus.

Many people believe that once someone gets filled with the Holy Ghost/Holy Spirit, that all those things are washed away, and we are a new creation in Christ. Yes! That is absolutely true and absolutely biblical. However, we are not void of struggle and temptation as long as we live in the world. Much of the struggles we go through come from within and are of our own making. Could those be due to generational strongholds? Generational ways of thinking? Generational traditions? Generational ways of doing life that brings about weight and sin in our lives, post our salvation experience?

I believe that is why Paul said in 1 Cor. 15:31, "I die daily." This was an act of free will, choosing to die to his fleshly impulses, needs and desires; walking in the spirit vs walking in the flesh. Paul then said in 2 Cor.10:4 "for the weapons of our warfare are not carnal, but mighty through God for the pulling down of strongholds, casting down imaginations, and every high thing that exalteth itself against the knowledge of God, bringing into captivity every thought to the obedience of Christ." This scripture is so powerful when you couple it with Proverbs 23:7 "as a man thinketh in his heart, so is he." Paul knew that thoughts produce emotion and emotion produces behavior, so Paul gives this instruction to the church in Corinth, who were already followers of Jesus.

There is much more to be said on the subject and this short essay cannot sufficiently convey my heart on this matter. What I am saying is this; people struggle with things in their lives after they have been saved, that can be identified throughout the family, in parents and grandparents. This prayer is for us to give God permission to the parts of our heart and mind that may be hidden from us, but not hidden from Him.

People often say "that is what I have always done," or "I have been this way my whole life." However, that doesn't mean that is who you are. God may want to remove some things from our lives if they are bringing about negative outcomes. While we pray this prayer asking God to break abuse cycles, let us add to the prayer, and ask Him to break any cycle that is negatively affecting us. Sometimes the cycles affecting our life is not always about sin. Sometimes it is a weight. Sometimes it is a sin.

So today, join me in praying this prayer and pray it over anyone you know that might be struggling with generational strongholds.

DAY 6

Lord, we ask that you would break every abuse cycle in our families. Break every cycle of sexual abuse physical abuse, and verbal abuse. Convict the hearts of the abusers and heal them. In Jesus name!

Declaration

We declare that God is breaking the abuse cycles in our families, and He is restoring the hearts of those that have been abused in Jesus name.

Chapter Seven
Leadership

Is this your experience, or should it be credited to someone else?

Living in Southern California taught me a lot of lessons. One such lesson was that the physical conditions around me can change in an instant.

In November 2018, I was sitting in my house, spending the evening with my family, when I noticed the wind was whipping around the house, rattling the windows. This wasn't strange, but the smell in the air was: thick, heavy, and smoky.

I went to the back door and tried to see if I could spot flames. High above the house behind us and above the hills beyond, red and yellow flames danced in the night sky.

This was the beginning of the Woolsey Fire. In a matter of days, this fire changed everything. It burned 96,949 acres of land, destroyed 1,643 homes, killed three people, and forced us to rethink where we wanted to live.

It seemed to come out of nowhere and consume the area in the blink of an eye. Black, dense smoke enveloped the streets. It poured into our home through every nook and cranny. We grabbed our three sons and our pet rabbit, jumped in our car, and headed out to a friend's house in Studio City.

We were forced to make decisions that night we never thought we'd have to make: what to leave in our house, when to flee, where to go, and how long to stay away.

We did the best we could with what we could see and discern. Smoke and flames make decision-making difficult though. In a second, the wind would kick up, and push the fire in another direction, causing confusion and chaos. No one can direct a fire—it tends to do what it wants to do. You have to respond to what it is doing, make the best decision you can for yourself and your family, and pray.

This chapter's prayer is for all the leaders of our cities to stand strong in the face of lies and deceptions. What is happening across the state is similar to a fire. Things have gotten out of control, fast. There continue to be many issues clouding the air, spiritually and morally, impacting everyone in every city. These raging fires in the hearts and minds of people produce disorienting thoughts, making decisions hard, forcing tough stands, and dividing communities. Cities could self-govern on many issues if they are willing to stand up against the state mandates. We witness this often in Huntington Beach, California.

The leaders across the state need God's help to see what is right and wrong. They need help cutting through the confusion and panic produced by issues not based on truth. They also need strength to face their fears of the potential fallout should they govern according to the constitutional rights of the people. We are praying that those who will not take a stand against the woke agenda will be removed and replaced with those who will.

DAY 7

Lord, lift up the leaders of our cities across California. Lord deal with their hearts & give them strength to stand for what is right. Give them strength to speak the truth in the face of lies and deception. Raise up new leaders who will follow your voice In Jesus name!

Declaration

Lord, thank you for the God-fearing leaders in our cities that you have given to us. We declare that our cities will be dominated by leaders chosen by you who will restore order and values throughout this state. In Jesus name.

Day Eight
Pray for Pastors

It seems that nothing shocks faithful churchgoers as much as a pastor falling into sin, leaving the ministry, or leaving the faith all together. It's stunning to us when the men and women who have taken on the call to shepherd God's people with His Word and Spirit trip up and fall to temptation. News of their fall spreads like wildfire. The tragic consequences of such a public scandal brings occasion for believers to move further away from God and deplete the faith in others.. Churches split. Homes are torn apart. The fallout is great. And yet it surprises us when it continues to happen.

But why? Pastors and ministers are flesh and blood, body and soul, wrestling with their sinful nature, just like us. Standing on a stage, behind a pulpit, proclaiming the word of God, does not lift them above the temptations and attacks of the enemy. They are fallible and bound to make mistakes in life, just like us.

Peter, Jesus' radical disciple, knew this better than anyone. 1 Peter 4:12 says, "Beloved, think it not strange concerning the fiery trial which is to try you, as though some strange thing happened unto you" (KJV). Fiery trials are part of the life of a believer and a pastor, but a lot of us have support systems, people we can rely on for prayer and guidance when we are tempted or when we fall down.

For pastors it is a bit more difficult. Who can they trust when they struggle or need to process something they are wrestling with? Many pastors don't often have the luxury of trusted friendships that allow them to be human and a pastor at the same time.

And it's having a deep impact.

Pastoral Care Inc. recently said that denominations are suffering under a shortage of ministers in an "Empty Pulpit Crisis." George Barna published stats showing that 42% of pastors thought of leaving their ministry in 2022. Nothing could illustrate the issues the pastors are facing as drastically as three prominent ministers committing suicide over the last four years—even as they were helping others with their mental issues.

Further on, Peter writes: "Be sober, be vigilant; because your adversary the devil walks about like a roaring lion, seeking whom he may devour. Resist him, steadfast in the faith, knowing that the same sufferings are experienced by your brotherhood in the world" (1 Peter 5:8-9 NKJV).

Just as we are to be sober and vigilant about our own walk, we believe God is asking us to be sober and vigilant for the men and women who have taken on the task of hearing from God and communicating with us every week.

The call for us all, and the prayer in this chapter, beckons us to remember the bullseye our pastors wear and to pray for them fervently and regularly.

DAY 8

Lord, we lift up every pastor across California. Strengthen them, Lord. Light a fire within them to earnestly seek you. Give them strength in body, mind, soul and spirit to do your will. In Jesus name!

Declaration

We bless every Pastor in California. We declare they will walk humbly before you and be led by your spirit only. In Jesus name.

Chapter Nine
Pray for Law Enforcement

When I was in my 20s, I spent two years working for my local police department. I would have become a police officer had God not intervened in my life two weeks prior to starting the police academy. I spent a lot of my free time riding along with the gang unit on weekends and had a front-row seat to the ins and outs of how law enforcement operated. I have the utmost respect for our law enforcement community.

Back then, 30 years ago, the average person still held law enforcement with high regard and respect. There were invisible lines that didn't get crossed by the criminally-inclined, or at least they were not crossed very often. But times have changed, and our law enforcement community is in the greatest danger they have probably ever been in in this generation.

As a clinician, I have worked with the families of police officers, and the officers themselves. For those not on the front lines, it is difficult to imagine what they actually experience. The level of depravity, the violence, parents and family members killing one another, and much more. Besides the ongoing threat of physical danger, they carry an enormous emotional weight that has lasting effects.

There is a famous psychological experiment that was conducted to test what makes people feel safe. The psychologist took some children, gave them toys, and put them in a house's backyard that ran right up to very busy train tracks.

The children investigated the yard, and wandered out into the grass, but quickly returned to the house when a train roared by, shaking the ground they walked on. For the rest of the day, they stayed near the patio and the back of the house.

Why? One thing was missing from this yard: a fence. Nothing separated them from the train and the tracks. They had complete freedom to roam and play, but there was no barrier to keep the train from them.

Later, they took the children, put them in another yard, gave them toys and free rein of the yard once again. Only this time, there was a fence. The psychologists watched as the children explored and played all over the yard, even right up to the fence, even with the train hurtling past them as before.

A simple fence gave the children enough of a security cushion that they could enjoy the freedom of playing, which a yard without a fence didn't allow.

We live in a free society. We can go and do and explore as much as we like, mostly without fear of danger. We do this every day because we have metaphorical fences around us: laws and law enforcement willing to protect us and keep us safe. Rarely do we stop and think about it, but without law and order, there is chaos, fear, and lawlessness; something the Bible says will occur in the last days. We are witnessing this now. Without peace officers in our midst, mostly unseen, we would be like the children in the yard with no fence, living with the threat of danger and never feeling safe.

I think we all grow used to the common and familiar. Just like so many other things in our lives, it is easy to take law enforcement for granted because we see it as a job they are getting paid for and law enforcement has been around for hundreds of years. But today, I want to draw attention to their humanity and remind us that God initiated law enforcement centuries ago (Romans 13).

When I wrote out the 30 days of prayer, I felt impressed to include the law enforcement community. I hope that as you pray this prayer with me, you will not only pray for their physical safety but also pray for their emotional safety, their marriages, and their children. I am so grateful for what they do day in and day out, and thankful for the contribution that community had on my life.

DAY 9

Lord, we thank you for peace officers who work to secure our families, businesses, farms, cities, counties, and highways. We ask that you protect them as they protect us. We ask that you keep them safe from those who want to harm them.
In Jesus name!

Declaration

Lord, we declare your divine protection over all peace officers across California, in Jesus name.

KATHY J. CHASTAIN

Chapter Ten
Forgiving

Offense is one of the biggest snares we all deal with as Christians. I don't know about you, but I am continually battling my thoughts where offense is concerned. Not because I am easily offended but because I am sensitive in my spirit and pick up on people's attitudes and dispositions easily. I have had to learn that people have instinctive initial reactions to things, and if I react to their first reaction because I recognize it is negative, I do them a disservice by not allowing them time to work through their own biases.

Just the other day, I had a wellness appointment at a specialist office that I had never been to before. I am an observer of details, and that day was no different. When I walked in, I was paying attention to every detail. The place was pristine and classically decorated. The staff was pleasant. Then, the nurse practitioner came in to greet me, and I am ashamed to say my instinctive reaction was not good. I am sure that person felt what I was feeling. My involuntary assessment was that they appeared very unprofessional in their overall appearance. I had a reaction that surprised me, and I didn't like it.

At the same moment, I thought to myself, "Why am I reacting this way? What is this in me that is causing me to react this way to this stranger who is here to provide a service to me?"

I have felt a similar reaction at times from clients entering my office for the first time. As soon as they walk in, I can feel their judgment or discomfort, and I do my best to disarm and be kind to them, knowing that their reaction to me is also instinctive for whatever reason.

I left the appointment that day wondering what was going on with me that caused such a negative reaction of judgment, and furthermore, how did I make that provider feel?

If we ask God to "search me…and see if there be any wicked way in me" (Psalms 139:23, 24 NKJV) he will do just that. God will show us what is in us if we will ask Him to, and lately he has been showing and refining me, which is what it is really all about - making us more like Him.

When I got home that day, I repented. I was ashamed of my behavior. I still have wounds that have produced perfectionistic traits, among other things. God has healed me in many areas, but I have been going through a new season of healing, which means old wounds are getting exposed. My reaction to the provider was about my own arrogance serving as a shield against old feelings of unworthiness. I had no idea that was still hidden in my heart until that experience.

Not only did I ask God to forgive me, I asked God to protect her from any negative feelings her interaction with me might have caused. I didn't want my behavior from unhealed wounds to have a negative effect on her. God can intervene and block what was said in nonverbal communication.

Perhaps you have been on the receiving end of someone's bad behavior and have become offended, or perhaps you have been the one acting in a manner that does not reflect the fruit of the spirit. Either way, we must give one another grace, while also granting ourselves grace which only comes when we forgive.

Today's prayer is a simple one. It is taken from Matthew 6:12-15: "Forgive our debts as we forgive our debtors…if we forgive men their trespasses, your heavenly father will also forgive you. But if you forgive not men their trespasses, neither will your heavenly father forgive you."

I think we forget, at times, that by holding offense against someone, God will not forgive us. That is a scary thing. I repent daily, just to be on the safe side. But there have been times I have been in prayer that the Lord brings up something that has been hidden away in the recesses of my heart, and when it comes up, I repent in a completely different way. I am sure you know what I am talking about.

Today, there may not be anything you need to ask forgiveness for. But I find when there is a willingness to forgive, sometimes that's all God requires. It is the posture of our heart that He is looking at. Maybe you need to forgive yourself, maybe you don't know how to forgive yourself, but if you are willing to do that, God will help you with the rest.

I will be seeing the provider soon, and when I do, I will apologize to her for how I treated her at our first meeting. I owe her that. I owe God that, and I owe myself that. In the middle of those two verses I quoted above is one very important key verse, sandwiched between three verses about forgiveness. "Lead us not into temptation but deliver us from evil."

I wonder if we are more prone to temptation because we have unforgiveness. Something to think about!

DAY 10

Lord, you said in your word, "forgive and you shall be forgiven" so Lord, I forgive every person who has wronged me. I forgive every person who has hurt and mistreated me. Lord, I forgive those who have been my enemy. In Jesus name!

Declaration

Lord, we have forgiven others so that we could be free and forgiven by you. We declare that all record of wrongdoing by us or against us has been wiped clean, In Jesus name.

GOD OF THE IMPOSSIBLE!

Chapter Eleven
Praying Against Suicide

This chapter was more difficult for me to write, due to several experiences I have had in this area. I had a hard time finding a good flow in the content because the subject matter is too vast to properly articulate in a short essay. It is also a subject that I have studied several times, and I still have much to learn on the matter. So, if this seems a bit jumbled, I apologize. I hope by the end you will understand a bit more of this very important subject.

It may be no surprise to you that teenagers struggle with self-hate, self-harm, and suicide. What may surprise you is the increase of this in younger children. I have seen this in clients as young as 7, 8, 9, and 10 years old. It is devastating to hear all the reasons kids believe they are bad, some with vivid ideas of how they would "murder" themselves, as one little kiddo said.

According to the California Department of Public Health, the number of emergency room visits for self-harm and suicide attempts in children aged 10-18 for the year 2021 was 1,153 per month or 38 per day. That is pretty severe.

For overall completed suicides in 2021, the ages 10-18 had 166 deaths, or 14 per month. That is 14 too many. Males overall have the highest number of deaths, and white males, in particular, have the highest number of deaths in any age group.

Self-injury, cutting, or self-mutilation is also on the rise. 17% of teenagers have reported recently harming themselves by cutting their skin, banging or hitting their head, or burning themselves. Adults are not immune: 5% of adults have admitted to hurting themselves in recent times. Self-injury is a way many cope to relieve painful or hard-to-express feelings.

Did you know that cutting and suicide are both found in scripture? Both were part of pagan worship. Blood holds significant symbolism in many religious and cultural practices, often representing life, sacrifice, and purification. In pagan traditions, blood might be used in rituals as an offering to deities or spirits, symbolizing a bond or covenant. In Christianity, blood holds deep significance, particularly in the context of Jesus Christ's sacrifice, symbolizing redemption and the forgiveness of sins. In various cultures, blood rituals are seen as a means of purification or as a way to establish a spiritual connection.

The starkest story of self-harm in the Bible was when Elijah faced off with the prophets of Baal on Mount Carmel, found in the book of 1 Kings 18:28. Elijah and the prophets of Baal were in a fight to see whose God was more powerful. The prophets of the false God Baal cut themselves as part of their unsuccessful attempt to summon their deity's attention, but their efforts were in vain. I am sure many of us have heard about and read that story many times, but did you ever notice that they cut themselves?

I have noticed in my therapy practice that it is boys who are most affected by self-hate and suicidal ideation, and girls are more inclined to cut themselves. Biblically speaking, it was boys who were marked for death by the kings on at least two occasions, once in the Old Testament and once in the New Testament. We know the stories: Moses was born during the slaughter of baby boys, and the promise of a messiah sent the king into a panic, causing another mass slaughter of baby boys to prevent the life of Jesus.

The Bible tells us in John 10:10 that the thief comes to steal, kill, and to destroy. Suicide and self-harm are the antithesis of humanity's most basic instinct, survival. So it begs the question, if our most visceral instinct is to live, where does suicide originate from? I believe it comes from the spirit world, a demonic attack against the very image of God that is found in every human. There is nothing that the enemy hates more than us because we are made in His image, and He loved us enough to die for us.

There is so much more to say on this subject, and if you are inclined, I encourage you to study the significance of blood. It is a powerful study that will give new meaning to the story of Adam, Eve, and the cross of Jesus.

I believe suicide and self-harm are spirits that we must pray against. Jesus came to bring life, and life more abundantly. Our kiddos are fighting against forces they know nothing about and losing daily, as are adults. They need us to stand in the gap and pray on their behalf. Only heaven will reveal what our prayer will do.

If you have intrusive thoughts of suicide or know someone who is struggling, please get into therapy, consult with your pastor or call or text the suicide hotline number at 988.

DAY 11

Lord, we ask that you rebuke the spirit of self-hate and suicide in our schools and among the youth in the State of California. We ask that you break the cycle of cutting and all forms of self-harm in our schools and among the Youth in the State of California. In Jesus name!

Declaration

Lord, we declare that the spirit of suicide and false identity that leads to self-hate will be eradicated in the state of California. We decree and declare that every cycle of self-harm has been broken by the power and the authority of the name of Jesus.

GOD OF THE IMPOSSIBLE!

Chapter Twelve
Generational Transfer

This chapter's prayer comes from Genesis 12:3. "I will bless those who bless thee and curse those who curse thee, and in thee, all the families of the earth shall be blessed."

When I wrote out these prayers last year, my focus was on seven main areas. As we go along, they may sound familiar, like this chapter's prayer about generational curses and generational blessings.

As the world continues its downhill spiral, these dichotomies seem more and more glaring. The line in the sand is getting wider and wider, the decay of humanity is morphing into something we haven't seen before, and the "do-gooders" seem to be a very small percentage, but that is looking at things through a worldly view. If we look at the world from a Biblical point of view, we know that Jesus has already made provisions for all things through the cross, and what is happening in the world today is no surprise.

The more I study my Bible, the clearer the dichotomies become. There is always a good and always an evil. Always what is right and true and always what is deceptive and wicked. Just read Ecclesiastes Chapter 3; it is full of dichotomies. Everything really does boil down to its simplest form. In the end, it is exactly as the Bible says it is. We are either living "for God or against him," there is no middle ground, and He has given us the ability to choose. Whether those choices are conscious or subconscious. We have free will.

Although generational curses and generational blessings are things that exist outside of our free will, we have the power to change the curses to blessings and the power to change the blessings to curses. It happens all the time. We are just not in the habit of looking at it from that lens.

To recap from a couple of chapters ago, a generational curse refers to negative patterns, behaviors, or circumstances that are believed to be passed down through family bloodlines, affecting multiple generations. These curses can manifest in various forms, including addiction, poverty, abuse, and dysfunctional relationships. Some attribute generational curses to spiritual or supernatural forces, while others view them as psychological or sociological phenomena. Generational curses may arise from unresolved trauma, unhealthy family dynamics, or societal influences. Traumatic experiences such as abuse, war, or natural disasters can leave lasting emotional scars that are transmitted from one generation to the next. Additionally, learned behaviors within families, such as substance abuse or destructive coping mechanisms, can perpetuate negative patterns across generations.

On the other hand, generational blessings are positive attributes, values, or achievements that are passed down through family lines. These blessings can include traits such as resilience, creativity, a strong work ethic, and a sense of community. Like generational curses, generational blessings can shape the lives and experiences of individuals and families across multiple generations. Cultivating generational blessings involves nurturing and reinforcing positive traits and values within the family unit. This can be achieved through open communication, role modeling, and the intentional transmission of family traditions and values. Celebrating achievements, fostering a supportive environment, and encouraging personal growth can further strengthen generational blessings and contribute to the well-being of future generations.

However, for those who were raised in dysfunctional families or abusive families, the deep psychological and emotional damage that perpetuates the cycles is not always easy to decipher. Those raised in functional homes can easily take it for granted because it is all they have ever known and there can lack real appreciation for the blessings one was born into.

I know for me, I had a bit of both. I was blessed to grow up in a home with two parents who took me to church and kept me safe from predators. We were an average middle-class family. Our home was both loving and "religious," and that created a lot of confusion for me. My parents were both first-generation Christians, and when they found the Lord, He changed their lives dramatically. So, they followed the church "rules" without a real understanding of the rules, which meant they could not always explain the rules to me. This formed a rebellion in me and a massive need to have my own voice. There is more to the story than that, but my point is that the good and the bad shape us in ways we don't always recognize. As I have gotten older, I have been able to connect the dots. I have grown to understand what the "rules" were intended for, and my parents settled into their relationship with the Lord, which only deepened with time. Also, I rejected the blessing and heritage I was born into for a time, and I am forever grateful for the goodness of God in his pursuit of me.

Today, pray this prayer over yourself and then stand in the gap for those who are unable to pray this prayer for themselves. Ask God to break and remove any generational curses and their effects, and ask God to bless you and bless those who have been a blessing to you. We can all do better at identifying the blessings in our life and living in gratitude. It is a game-changer!

DAY 12

Lord, we ask you to break every generational curse that continues to be passed through families. Break generational addiction, poverty, criminality, premature death and sickness. Bring generational blessing to these families and change their future. In Jesus name!

Declaration

Lord, we declare that generational curses have been broken off my life and generational blessings will bring confirmation, in Jesus name.

GOD OF THE IMPOSSIBLE!

Chapter Thirteen
Setting Cities Free

This prayer is a powerful tool to keep our cities rid of influences that further demoralize our culture.

City managers, council members, and county boards of supervisors have the power to allow or block businesses such as psychics, strip clubs, casinos, card rooms, marijuana dispensaries, and abortion clinics, just to name a few. In my city, our city council is made up of five people, and our board of supervisors is made up of five people. Those 10 people decide what will or will not be allowed into my community. Your town is not much different.

Many of these establishments already exist in most cities and counties around California, but that doesn't mean things can't change. Those entities bring with them demonic forces that begin to influence culture wherever they are.

However, when Godly leaders step up and speak out, standing up for family values, morality, and righteousness, cities can be set free, city leaders can be influenced in a Godly way, and the people living in those areas can experience a better quality of life. Just look at Philip, Paul, and Silas's impact on their cities.

We see in Acts 8 and Acts 16 that spirits operating through individuals, controlled towns and businesses, oppressing them and holding them back from the truth of Jesus Christ.

In Acts 8, we see that a man's demonic spirit controlled an entire city:

"But there was a certain man called Simon, who previously practiced sorcery in the city and astonished the people of Samaria, claiming that he was someone great, to whom they all gave heed, from the least to the greatest, saying, '"This man is the great power of God.'" And they heeded him because he had astonished them with his sorceries for a long time" (Acts 8:9-11 NKJV).

In Acts 16, we see Paul and Silas confronting a fortune-telling slave girl, setting her free in the name of Jesus, and the fallout from it: the businesses had them arrested and put in jail.

Whenever spirits of this type are allowed to operate openly, evil and decay follow in their wake.

As we pray, we DO NOT pray against the businesses operating in our cities and counties. That is a subject matter all its own. We must pray for the individuals who have the authority to make the decisions. Then let God do the rest!

Our City and County leaders are just people who can be influenced for good. If you do not know the leaders of your community, call their office and make an appointment to meet with them. Get to know them. Let them know you are praying for them. Encourage them. You will feel good about it, and so will they!

DAY 13

Lord, we ask that you convict City Council members and county Board of Supervisors from approving strip clubs, psychic businesses, and card rooms from opening in our cities and counties. We also ask Lord, that our city and county leaders would be inspired to build safe and wholesome family friend environments. In Jesus name!

Declaration

We declare that you, Lord are returning our cities and counties back to family-friendly environments because you have changed the hearts of our leaders, in Jesus name.

Chapter Fourteen
Wolves in Sheeps Clothing

"There once was a certain wolf who could not get enough to eat because of the watchfulness of the shepherds. But one night, he found a sheepskin that had been cast aside and forgotten. The next day, dressed in the skin, the Wolf strolled into the pasture with the Sheep. Soon, a little Lamb followed him about and was quickly led away to be devoured by the wolf."

This is the beginning of the famous Aesop's Fable. It is a familiar fable and we have heard one version or another of this tale. It is part of our culture, with secular and Christian leaders referencing it.

As a young girl, I grew up with such a wolf in sheep's clothing.

Before I was born, my mom was invited to church by a coworker. Mom grew up in a small-town Methodist church and swore to herself she would never go to church once she became an adult. But her coworker was full of Jesus and my mom observed that her friend seemed happy, and my mom definitely was not.

After mom attended that first service with her friend, she brought my dad with her to the next service. He had not been raised in church and he did not know if God was real. That night at church, he said a simple prayer, "God if you are real, show me" and immediately, my father's hands began to shake, and he felt the presence of the Lord all over him.

They were both on fire for Jesus! They raised my sister and I in this church. As little girls, we went to church twice on Sundays, with church lasting very late into the evening, and several times throughout the week. It was a Pentecostal spirit-filled church and as a child, I witnessed many miracles and healings. People were also being delivered from addiction on a regular basis. Church was an exciting place to be, and I loved it! Our church believed in the nine gifts of the spirit as described in 1 Corinthians 12 and the church began to move deeper into the prophetic ministry (something I believe in and something I think is absolutely needful for this day and hour we are living in). Soon the pastor brought in a prophet from Texas to hold revivals. He was coming very regularly and there was an air of expectation to see what God would do.

It wasn't long before the truth of what was happening in the dark was exposed. As it happened, the pastor and the prophet were frequently taking trips to Los Angeles and to Las Vegas, paying prostitutes and hosting other women in a secret condo in Los Angeles, spending the money from the building fund. The pastor was also involved in an extra marital affair with a lady in the church. Around the same time, it came out that the male piano player and the male choir director were involved with one another, both of whom were married to women. It was a scandalous mess. I was 11 when my parents and several other families left the church.

Jesus, in his Sermon on the Mount, spoke of false Christian leaders. "Beware of false prophets, who come to you in sheep's clothing, but inwardly they are ravenous wolves" (Matthew 7:15 NKJV).

As a Christian Based Psychotherapist, I have worked with many in the church world and have heard horrific stories of abuse and narcissistic personalities behind the pulpit who manipulate and intimidate their members with a religious spirit, a deadly combination which the Bible calls witchcraft.

GOD OF THE IMPOSSIBLE!

The Bible teaches us to "test the spirits to see whether they are from God, for many false prophets are gone out into the world" (1 John 4). The spirit world is real, prophets are real, which is why there can be false prophets. The Bible also tells us that "we will know them by their fruit" (Matt 7: 16-20).

We must not limit the gifts of the Holy Ghost/Spirit from operating in the church, but we must walk circumspectly and test the spirit and be sure that a person's life operating in the prophetic is bearing the fruit of the spirit. The prophetic movement has taken center stage in some circles, and it is needful, but listen closely to the people you follow on YouTube. If they promote self, beware. Humility is often what I look for. But all of us must trust the Spirit of the Lord that lives in us to properly discern.

In this chapter's prayer, we are asking God to expose and remove those who do not present themselves as they really are. Those who are hiding behind a false identity. Those who are wolves, being led by the wrong spirit.

The end of the fable talks about the Shepherd unknowingly saving his sheep by mistaking the wolf who is in a sheep's skin for the sheep. "That evening, the Wolf entered the fold with the flock. But the shepherd took a fancy for mutton broth that evening and, picking up a knife, went to the fold. The first animal he laid hands on and killed was the Wolf."

Thankfully, we have a real Shepherd who is always vigilant, always on guard, and always watching out for us. He can protect us from much of the evil the enemy wants to do in the church when we walk in the spirit.

This is a time when the ministry needs prayer more than ever. As you pray for the exposure and removal of the wolves, please also pray for the ministry leaders who are ministering from the truth of God's word.

DAY 14

Lord, expose every wolf in sheep's clothing in the churches across California. Expose them and remove them. Undo every evil deed that they perpetrated on your people and bring them to a place of repentance that they may be forgiven and saved. In Jesus name!

Declaration

Lord, we declare your mercy over every wolf in sheep's clothing. We decree and declare the fear of the Lord will cause them to repent and make their life right with you, in Jesus name.

GOD OF THE IMPOSSIBLE!

Chapter Fifteen
That Truth Comes to Light

We live in a time when so many parents are not parents, and families are families in name only. I am so thankful for those of you who are suiting up and showing up in a parental role. You are making a difference.

Children today are living in a world of unprecedented evil. The number of people who abuse and neglect their children is, sadly, the majority, based on the research. I am thankful for the hand of God, who watches over and protects our loved ones.

This prayer is for investigators, those whose job it is to determine the truth from a lie, those whose hands are often tied with protocol; and ever changing laws that prevent law enforcement from doing the job of justice. The constraints placed on law-enforcement must be frustrating for our men and women who wear the badge, who become important to the victim and their families.

In 2017, I opened a Runaway Homeless Youth Shelter for girls 12-18. The shelter originated with a young girl I taught Bible study to in a juvenile detention facility. As a result of this case, and many others, I have experienced both sides of the investigative process.

I have been involved in child welfare cases where the investigators were extremely closed-minded and biased and in other cases where investigators diligently sought and fought for the truth. I cannot blame those who have become jaded; the world is cruel, and that line of work exposes them to the ugliest parts of humanity. But we need them, and we need them to have their own level of integrity that will rise up and do what is right, even when they don't feel the truth or evidence will make a difference.

The Bible says that truth is a spirit. It also says that fear is a spirit, as is wisdom, infirmity, lying, and many other manifestations a person can exhibit. In John 16:13, the Bible says, "However, when He, the Spirit of truth, has come, He will guide you into all truth; for He will not speak on his own authority, but whatever He hears He will speak; and He will tell you things to come."

The spirit of truth is the Lord; as the Bible says, "God is a spirit."

I have prayed many times for the Lord to reveal the truth to someone so that the truth would abide with them and counter-act whatever lies the adversary would whisper in their ears, allowing the truth to prevail. I especially prayed this over my son as he was growing up. There were many, many circumstances that could have easily turned his heart away from me, but I prayed, above all else, that the Lord would love him in my absence and that he would know the truth of his mother's heart. I know the Lord answered those prayers.

I believe we can pray that same prayer and other prayers over the investigators across our state.

Today's prayer is a call to action, reminding us that these men and women fighting for the truth need our prayers and God's help. Please, take a moment today to lift them up in prayer, just as you would your son or daughter, mother or father, friend or neighbor. Who knows what lives will be saved and changed by this simple little prayer.

DAY 15

Lord, we pray for every investigator who represents law enforcement agencies, District Attorney's offices, Public Defender's offices, and all state investigators, reveal the truth to them in each situation. Let them pursue the truth and only the truth. Let them be men and women of integrity. In Jesus name!

Declaration

Lord, we declare your truth is flowing out of every investigator across the state. We decree and declare they will be men and women of integrity, in Jesus name.

Chapter Sixteen
Healing from the Inside-Out

This prayer is one I pray almost daily. It is a prayer for healing. Most people think of healing as physical healing, but when I wrote this prayer, I was thinking of emotional and soul healing. However, there is a link between wounds of the soul and physical disease.

The soul is comprised of our mind, our will, and our emotions. Our thoughts, desires, and emotions dictate our behaviors. This is Cognitive-Behavioral Therapy in a nutshell.

As babies, we come into this world whole, pure, innocent, unfiltered. Then life begins, and little by little, through a frustrated adult raising their voice, a toddler stealing a toy at daycare, or a friend at school being mean for no apparent reason, wounds begin to form in the heart. Over time, the innocence is gone, and the heart starts to splinter and fragment.

These wounds form our biases, proclivities, values, morals, and desires. Some of the hurts of childhood we consider to be "normal" and therefore accept, not realizing that there was an actual wound. The memories of these incidents get buried and forgotten, and with traumatic pain, the psyche can blackout memories altogether.

I see this in my work, and it was also true for me.

When we bury our wounds, or unknowingly create a dissociative wall, we do not always recognize our need for healing, but there are always symptoms pointing us to the need for inner healing. Here are a few ways unhealed wounds manifests physically and emotionally.

- Addiction
- Disease
- Flashbacks/Nightmares
- Emotionally Numb
- Self-Destructive Behavior
- Sexually Avoidant/ Sexually Promiscuous
- Obesity
- People Pleasing
- Conflict Avoidant
- Perpetual Anger/Rage
- Impulsivity

All of us are doing the best we can with the environment we grew up in. Some of us are still surviving, and some of us are thriving.

Whatever place you find yourself in, there will always be more layers to be healed, not because there is necessarily something wrong, but because the Lord is constantly molding us to be more like Him.

I am now in my mid-fifties and in another season of healing. Just when I think I am in a "good" place because I have fought and won most of the battles, a new season of healing begins. I have come to know that when we go through these seasons, it is because of God's goodness and love for us. As He reveals and heals the areas of hurt in our hearts, He also corrects how we view others and the world around us.

GOD OF THE IMPOSSIBLE!

Every group we have been praying for during the 30 days and chapter prayers is comprised of people like you and me who need healing. Today's prayer asks the Lord to heal us as individuals, heal our marriages, and heal our families.

DAY 16

Lord, we ask that you heal us. Heal our hearts, all our wounds from childhood to now. Heal our families, heal our marriages, and give us supernatural grace to love those around us. In Jesus name!

Declaration

Lord, we declare your healing over our hearts, childhood wounds, marriages and our families. You have healed us, and you are healing us with each passing day. In Jesus name.

Chapter Seventeen
Loneliness, Rejection & Abandonment

Loneliness, rejection, and abandonment are three of the toughest emotions to process, cope with, and heal from. I have struggled with them at different times in my life and went through great agony surviving and healing from those debilitating emotions.

Some people do not always survive.

I don't know where I would be today if I had not known the Lord through those times. I often wonder how anyone survives the hardships of life without a relationship with Jesus. Life can be so brutally tragic.

The emotional state of loneliness is a complex, and a deeply felt experience that transcends mere physical isolation. It is characterized by a perceived gap between the social connections one desires and those that are actually present. This perception can lead to a profound sense of emptiness, worthlessness, and alienation.

Emotionally, loneliness often manifests as sadness and a persistent feeling of being disconnected from others, even in a crowded room or surrounded by acquaintances and sometimes even when surrounded by family or spouses. This sense of disconnection can stem from a lack of meaningful relationships, where interactions fail to fulfill an individual's emotional needs. Consequently, loneliness can breed feelings of being misunderstood, unsupported, and unloved.

Researcher and author Brené Brown says that loneliness is the absence of belonging–the absence of belonging to others, belonging to something, or belonging to our own sense of self.

The emotional pain associated with loneliness can trigger a range of psychological responses.

For some, it leads to heightened anxiety and constant worry about social interactions and relationships. This anxiety can further isolate individuals as they might avoid social situations to prevent rejection or further emotional distress.

Loneliness also impacts self-esteem and self-worth. People often internalize their social struggles, attributing their loneliness to personal deficiencies or unworthiness. This negative self-perception can create a self-reinforcing cycle, where the fear of rejection and the belief in one's own inadequacy prevent the formation of new connections and deepen the sense of isolation.

When I think of loneliness, I think it could be the closest thing to being in hell that we will ever experience in this life. I know that is a dramatic statement, but the Bible speaks of hell as total darkness, the absence of light, the absence of love, and ultimately, the absence of God, who is light and love. The complete loss of connection to anything or anyone. Alone, forever.

I see loneliness as a byproduct of abandonment and/or rejection.

Abandonment refers to the emotional experience of being left behind or deserted by someone significant, such as a family member, friend, or partner. For children, this often happens as a result of a divorce. This experience can be particularly traumatic and leave long-lasting emotional scars. Abandonment exacerbates loneliness by instilling a fear of future desertion, making individuals hesitant to form new attachments. The fear of abandonment can lead to clinginess or withdrawal in relationships, both of which can perpetuate a cycle of loneliness and isolation.

Rejection involves dismissing or refusing someone's thoughts, feelings, or presence. It can occur in various contexts, such as social, romantic, or professional interactions. Experiencing rejection can intensify feelings of loneliness, as it directly undermines an individual's sense of belonging and acceptance. The emotional pain of rejection often leads to heightened self-awareness and self-criticism, reinforcing the belief that one is unworthy of connection, thereby deepening the sense of loneliness. This can also occur for children when their parents divorce. Children can feel so insignificant to one or the other parent when a divorce occurs, but rarely do they have the tools to understand or express the deep sense of loss they experience. What they do express is, "If only I was better."

When these three experiences combine, they create a powerful feedback loop, also known as a cycle. Loneliness makes individuals more vulnerable to acutely feeling the sting of rejection and abandonment. In turn, experiences of rejection and abandonment validate and deepen the feelings of loneliness. This cyclical relationship can result in chronic loneliness, where the individual struggles to break free from the emotional and psychological impacts of these experiences.

I do not have to tell you all the ways in which our kiddos are struggling in today's society. But what I didn't know, and am learning more through the course of my work and personal experiences, is the profound impact divorce has on children. I think, all too often, we accept divorce as a part of life and minimize it as adults because several of us have been through it, and as adults going through a divorce, we are dealing with our own loss and struggles when it happens. We assume our kids will be ok, and perhaps, in time they will be, but perhaps the wounds they bare are far greater than we know.

Think about all the kiddos throughout our state who have had their families torn apart due to divorce, or who do not have attentive parents, or do not have parents at all due to incarceration, death, removal by CPS, or other such things. Think about the kiddos who have never been introduced to a God who loves them, who created them in His image. How will these kids deal with loneliness, abandonment, and rejection?

We already know that answer.

Today, I hope you will feel a burden for the youth of California, and the youth around the world for that matter. I hope that burden will inspire lasting prayer for them. Pray that God will supernaturally and miraculously draw them into a relationship with Him. He is the healer, the comforter, the great lover of our soul, and the answer they need.

DAY 17

Lord, we ask that your love would reach the children and youth throughout California. We pray for hearts that are lonely, and hearts that have been broken by rejection and abandonment. Heal them all by your loving kindness. In Jesus name!

Declaration

Lord you are Love. We receive your love. We declare that the youth of California is feeling your love even now. We decree and declare that rejection, abandonment, and loneliness will leave our youth, in Jesus name.

Chapter Eighteen
The Difficulty of Marriage & the Fight to Stay Together

I recently heard a quote by Dr. Gary Lawrence that I loved. I loved it because it is so accurate, even if at first it feels discouraging. The quote is:

"Opposites attract, then they attack, then they retract."

The saying "opposites attract" is often used to describe how people with different traits or qualities can be drawn to one another. There are several psychological, biological, and sociological reasons why this might happen:

1. Complementary Traits: People with opposite traits can complement each other. For example, a person who is very outgoing may feel balanced and grounded by someone who is more introverted and calm.

2. Novelty and Excitement: Opposite traits can introduce novelty and excitement into a relationship. Differences can keep things interesting and help partners learn new perspectives and experiences.

3. Biological Factors: From an evolutionary standpoint, genetic diversity can be beneficial. Some studies suggest that individuals may be subconsciously attracted to others with different immune system genes, which could lead to healthier offspring.

4. Psychological Balance: Opposites may attract because they provide psychological balance. A person might seek out traits in a partner that they feel they lack in themselves, creating a sense of completeness.

5. Social and Cultural Influences: Social and cultural narratives often romanticize the idea of opposites attracting and influencing people to seek out relationships that fit this pattern.

However, while opposites may initially attract, that doesn't mean they are compatible. Often, people can be attracted to someone because they share a common thought, belief, or behavior derived from a wounded heart that they see in themselves. It feels like a real connection, but in fact, it is a familiar emotion and not real connectedness. It is more about relatability, empathy, or sympathy, but those emotions are not the same as connection when it comes to being able to build a romantic foundation of love. It may feel amazing, but only time will tell if it will be real and lasting.

Soon enough into the relationship, reality sets in, and so do our differences. This is one reason we hear so much about communication being key to a successful relationship. Most of us were raised in a reward/punishment dichotomy. The psychological term is "classical conditioning," which means, "if we do something good, we get something good, and if we do something bad, we will get something bad." It is an either/or scenario. It's black or white, right or wrong. Nothing in between. So, when couples disagree or have conflict, generally speaking, someone has to be wrong while the other person is right. Incidentally, this is also how a lot of people view God. He is either a good God or a punishing God. However, neither of those assumptions is correct. There is ALWAYS more!

Two people can be right at the same time. Two people can be wrong at the same time, and one person can be right while the other is wrong, but that doesn't mean they had ill intent or had ulterior motives. A person's heart can be in the right place and still do something their spouse would deem as wrong. I am so thankful God looks at our heart and takes into consideration our motive. We should do the same for our spouses.

When it comes to marriages attacking each other, I have observed some common ways men and women attack one another, aside from the obvious abusive cycles.

The common complaints men have about their wives are: the wife is too critical and tends to assassinate the husband's character, and/or she withholds sex and neglects physical intimacy.

The common complaints women have about their husbands are that they don't help enough with household duties, that their husbands emotionally withdraw, and that they lack or stop communicating with them.

Once these negative cycles begin, over time, marriage can feel more like an obligation rather than love, and retraction easily begins. In marriage and in Christianity, obligation never works for very long. The only thing that will ever work is love because love motivates us toward goodwill to our object of affection. Love can only come through a person's ability to choose. It is the entire reason God created us with free will. He wants us to choose him from a position of love and not obligation. It is the only way a marriage will ever last and the only way our relationship with Jesus remains pure.

To say that love is the tie that binds is cliché, but it is true. I have worked with many couples, and I can always tell when a couple has a bond of love, even if it is buried deeply under all the problems. A foundation of love is necessary to build a relationship, and long-term compatibility often depends on shared values, goals, and interests. In this sense, being attracted to one's opposite may not be optimal because similarity is needed for longevity.

Marriage is probably the most difficult thing any of us will ever have to do if it is going to last and be fulfilling. The old adage that says "marriage is work" is 100% true. Those who are willing to die for themselves in order to love another will do the work (that is not the same as being a doormat and being abused). Those who are not willing to sacrifice self will not make it through marriage. That is a simple and provable fact, and sadly, the vast majority of people are not willing to do the work because it is just too easy to blame the other person or quit. But please know it takes two people to be married. Let me say that again. It takes two people to make a marriage work. You cannot make a marriage work one-sided. That is a topic for a different day.

I was one of those people. I chose myself over others for reasons I have only understood in the past 10 years. I have learned that marriage is meant to be a reflection of our walk with God. To ultimately reveal what it means to be in a covenant relationship with Him. To remain faithful to Him in the midst of hurt, confusion, and disappointment. To learn what it means to forgive often and to be forgiven. To be in love with Him and stay in relationship with Him through life's hardships. To be obedient to the word of God, His word. To believe the best about Him and know that He is working for our good when circumstances look different.

I wonder what would happen if we reexamined 1 Corinthians 13 and endeavored to love Jesus and our spouses in the way love is defined in that chapter. It isn't easy, that is for sure. But it does quickly reveal where pride is hidden, where fear exists, where selfish ambition and motives are hidden.

Marriage is an opportunity for the Lord to reveal in us all the hidden places in our heart that keep us bound and living with less than what He has for us. Imagine if marriages across our state and across the U.S. would pray for each other and begin to love one another in the way God intended, how our country, our state and our children would change. We would see a revival of family and a revival of morality.

At the end of the day, one person can make a difference. Because one person becomes two people and two people become three people. If each of us would do our own individual part with what God has entrusted us with, everything would change.

It begins with you; it begins with me. Will you pray for marriages today, and will you endeavor to love your people according to the Biblical definition of love?

DAY 18

Lord, we ask that you restore the family unit in California. Raise up fathers and mothers who will love and serve their children. Restore marriage between a man and a woman, fill homes across California with a conviction to stay married and work on unity instead of division.
In Jesus name!

Declaration

Lord, we declare the restoration of families and marriages throughout California. We declare a revival of your love to sweep our state, in Jesus name.

GOD OF THE IMPOSSIBLE!

Day Nineteen
Removal of Corrupt Politicans

I am excited about this prayer! I have been a witness to some pretty incredible miracles recently and I am more convinced than ever of the miraculous power of God.

I had a conversation this week with a friend who said, "I will pray, but it doesn't look good." I know that sentiment is shared by many; as we watch the world changing in such drastic ways on a daily basis, sometimes it feels like it is changing every hour. We have watched as our constitution is ignored, our justice system has become yet another branch of corruption, and the powers that be seemingly get away with blatant lies and deceit. It has been shocking, to say the least. I cannot blame anyone for being discouraged by all that is going on in the world today.

But as the time approached for me to sit down and write about this chapter's prayer, I felt a holy fight stir within me, and I was reminded of what I felt in my spirit when I wrote my book, "Redeem California, With God, All Things Are Possible." That book was written from a profound revelation of who WE are in Christ. WE have the power, not the enemy. The enemy is just screaming the loudest. But that is what the enemy does; he works through lies and intimidation. That may be working for a while, but the lies are getting exposed. There are those of us who know who we are in God, and we understand this battle belongs to the Lord!!! We are slowly letting our voices be heard!

I am not going down without a fight! California and the United States belong to God Almighty, and we, the people of God, are the victors of this battle because that is who God made us to be!!! It is NOT just a fantasy or whimsical thought. It is a reality written across the pages of scripture. We may not be crossing the Red Sea or marching around the walls of Jericho, but God has not changed. He is the same God today as He was way back then. When the people of God inquired of the Lord, not only did He answer them, but He also went before them in battle and defeated the enemy for them. He commanded them to take territory because it was their promised land. He cleared the path and gave them the strategy; all they had to do was obey. Over and over again throughout the Old Testament, the deciding point of Israel's ability to defeat their enemy was whether or not they were following and obeying the Lord.

The enemy has taken prayer out of schools; he has stolen the rainbow. He has stolen gender identity; he has shed innocent blood and profaned some of the most beautiful cities in California that were named after saints. Cities that were established to further the gospel. Well, I want it all back. We all want it all back, and the Bible says the enemy must repay seven times whatever he has stolen. I am looking for my/our payback.

But more than all of that, I am excited because I know God is who He says He is, and He will do what He said He will do. He will "bind up the brokenhearted, open the eyes of the blind, set at liberty the captives, and preach the gospel to the poor" (Luke 4:18). When God pours out His Spirit over our state, the wicked will have to bow to His name, and those who have been vessels in the hand of the wicked one will have a heart- change that will transform our state in ways people don't think possible. But I believe God will do the impossible, and I think you also believe!

GOD OF THE IMPOSSIBLE!

Our battle is not with flesh and blood but against principalities, powers, rulers of the darkness of this world, and against spiritual wickedness in high places. (Eph 6:12). Prayer is our weapon. Let's call on the name of Jesus together and watch God do the impossible in California and in our United States.

DAY 19

Lord, we ask that you eradicate the wickedness and evil agenda coming through the legislative body in California. Remove every corrupt politician in California and raise up new leaders who will uphold our constitutional rights.
In Jesus name!

Declaration

Lord, we declare that all wicked and evil agendas that have come through our legislative body in California will be eradicated and that every corrupt politician in California will be removed in Jesus name. We further declare new leaders will rise up who will uphold our constitutional rights, In Jesus name.

GOD OF THE IMPOSSIBLE!

Chapter Twenty
The Heart of People

My heart has been heavy the past several days. Last week I received news of a young person that I used to see often, had lost their life to suicide, and it broke my heart. I have had so many thoughts, feelings and frustration as a result of this loss. It is incredibly sad and unnecessary. I am reminded once again of how desperately the world needs Jesus.

There have been times in my work, when I have sat with my clients, feeling utterly helpless to help them. The things that people go through are heartbreaking, and sometimes there are no words that will comfort or help and so I hold space for them and listen.

In those times, I have to remind myself that I am not their savior; I can only listen, support, and guide. It is a horrible feeling, seeing the depth of pain in another but not able to get through to them. The only thing that will ever help the truly broken and wounded soul is Jesus.

Sadly, so many people feel as if even God can't help. I don't know if it is because they have not encountered a truly loving Christian or if they have become so disillusioned from unanswered prayers. I am sure there are many other reasons why people's faith that God will help has diminished, but the bottom line is that it simply isn't true. When people fail to believe that God is the answer, they are left with the lie that something else is the answer.

When I started Redeem California, I had big plans to inspire faith in the hearts of those who love the Lord. I still feel that disappointment and hope deferred has caused the hearts of many to become discouraged and without hope.

I wanted to expose the lies of the enemy that would cause believers to question whether or not God was still on His throne and bring awareness to all the other issues we see taking place in our schools, our legal system, our families and our country. I thought people needed to know what was happening before our very eyes and I thought that pastors need to talk about all this from the pulpit.

I quickly realized everyone had their own agendas, and even people with huge platforms of influence weren't able to get through to those who didn't want to listen. I became discouraged myself and thought maybe I had missed God. I was so convinced he had called me to this mission of Redeeming California, but no one seemed to want to listen. Then I realized after much time and tears that I was powerless and once again surrendered this mission and message to the Lord. In surrendering, I understood that Redeem California is His burden; I am simply a vessel He is using.

My point is that disappointment comes, and things do not always go as planned, but it doesn't mean we stop believing, hoping, fighting, and enduring.

The level of trauma some people go through is nothing short of evil perpetrated on them by people who, in my opinion, are under the influence of demonic forces. It is sad and awful, and the system does little to help.

While we cannot control what happens to us in life, we can control the way we respond to what happens. There are injustices that make forgiveness difficult. An unexpected death of a loved one, betrayal, disease, sickness, abuse, financial hardship, and more. None of these things are ok, yet they will happen because we live in a fallen world, and the Lord told us in his Word that we would have trouble. But it is our response that determines what will happen when the trouble passes. If we fail to forgive, if we fail to surrender our heart to the Lord, if we fail to let God fight our battles, then we open the door for hatred, strife, and unbelief, all of which end in death, both physical and spiritual.

There is no room for us, as Christians, to hold offense against person or situation. None! We destroy our own souls if we do not submit our hurt to the Lord and allow him into those places in our hearts.

I am sure many of you have suffered injustice, slander, betrayal, abuse or loss. You probably have every right to feel justified in your anger, believing the person who hurt you doesn't deserve to be forgiven. You would be right.

However, we did not deserve to be forgiven when Jesus gave his life for ours. Whatever hurt you, whoever hurt you, God saw every bit of it. Those people belong to Him, and we must surrender them to the Lord. If we refuse to surrender those things to the Lord, we tie His hands. We prevent Him from moving in that situation because we are holding it in our own hands.

Maybe God has not answered the prayers prayed in times of great need, and you believe that he does not care or is not listening. That happened to me when I was 15 years old and I didn't know what to do with my disappointment. Up until that time, I believed God for the impossible and I believed He would answer whatever prayer I prayed. I was dismayed and confused by his lack of response to my heartfelt and sincere cries of desperation.

Now, all these years later, I have realized there was much I did not know about God. Much I did not know about His word, and much I didn't understand about His process of development. Those prayers he did not answer when I was 15, were eventually answered, and answered at a time when I could accept and understand the answer.

We cannot always see the hand of God working, but if we live long enough, EVERYTHING begins to make sense and everything receives an answer. God always answers, just not always in our timing. We must believe, from the depth of our soul, that God is good and His ways are perfect. If we believe that and do not waver , the trials we face will be much easier to endure because He is faithful, and blessings follow every time.

I encourage you to look at your life and see if there are any places that you have been disappointed, and are sad or angry without resolution or answer. Surrender all those places to the Lord and repent for holding any doubt or unbelief.

I repent daily to stay in a place of surrender and humility, lest any root of bitterness set in. The devil is sly and slithery and things can come in without us even realizing it. I have been shocked within myself at all the ways unbelief and pride has shown up in my life.

After the suicide of this young person, I haven't been able to get away from the convicting desire to see the devil defeated. I hated him before, and I hate him now, with a righteous hate for his tactics to steal, kill, and destroy humans.

I am convinced now more than ever that the only thing that is going to transform California and the United States is the love of God, Christians fighting through prayer and reaching people, one person at a time.

Then we will see California and the United States transformed.

DAY 20

Lord, stir the hearts of your people across the state of California. Draw them back to their first love, which is you and renew their purpose in you. Fill them full of your spirit and cause their light to shine bright in the darkness around them.
In Jesus name!

Declaration

Lord, we declare that you are drawing the cold and lukewarm Christian back to their first love, you. And you are renewing their purpose with a light that shines bright for you.
In Jesus name.

Chapter Twenty-One
Discernment Over Being Politically Correct

This prayer is for the police officers working in our school system. Police Officers need a lot of prayer overall, but especially the ones who work so closely with our children.

I am not sure how many of you have followed the changes the legislative branch has made regarding law enforcement, but the government in California has restricted what police officers can and cannot do since 2016, and especially since 2023. The way in which law enforcement actually police has been greatly restricted. They are not free to serve and protect without constant scrutiny and the fear of being sued

Being a police officer used to be a position of honor and respect. There was a code on the street that whatever criminal behavior someone engaged in, it was never ok to kill a cop or a clergy member. There was a reverence then that does not exist today. In today's society, law enforcement officers are in constant danger and are frequently murdered from sheer hatred of the uniform. We are truly living in a lawless society and are in need of police officers now more than ever. Law enforcement officers need our support and prayer to perform their jobs without fear of reprisal.

When I hear about a school shooting, I know it could have been avoided if those close to the situation had trusted their instincts and implemented preventative measures. Unfortunately, the system doesn't operate like that. Similar to doctors, those in the school setting and child welfare services can only treat the symptom and even then, the symptom requires evidence. If there is no proof, nothing happens.

When an officer is appointed to a school campus, that officer has years of experience under their belt. They know human behavior, and they have become good at profiling, not because of prejudice but because of years of experience. Again, it is no different from a doctor who treats someone for the flu, kidney infection, or any other ailment. They can spot it a mile away if they have been doing it long enough. But because of the restrictions placed on them by our government, many police officers' hands are tied.

My goal with this chapter's prayer is that our law enforcement community will bravely follow their instinct to help our kids while on school campuses instead of being politically correct. They know the kids who struggle, they know the kids who have bullied other kids, they see the kids who have been bullied, they know the kids who have attempted suicide, they know the kids who are being abused at home, or raised in a home with active addiction These are the kids who need help! They know but they can't always act, or they choose to be safe rather than suffer a negative consequence. I can't really blame them, but things are becoming more and more dangerous as the days go by, and one of our first lines of defense protecting our children while they are at school is the campus police officers.

So today, we ask God to give them a greater level of discernment so that they will have the strength and courage to do what is right, even if it means they may get in trouble for doing the right and good thing.

DAY 21

Lord, we pray for every police officer that works on school campuses. Give them discernment to sense danger and discernment to know when a student is struggling or in danger at home. Give them eyes to see and ears to hear what they need to know to protect our children and keep them safe. In Jesus name!

Declaration

Lord, we declare that our school police officers will have an increased level of discernment to sense danger before it happens with the students they protect. In Jesus name.

Chapter Twenty-Two
Humility

Humility could be one of the most difficult postures for the average human. It is definitely not my strong suit, but one I am working on. I find it much easier to humble myself before the Lord than I do with people. I trust the Lord, but people are far more difficult to trust. That is because people have hurt me; no doubt, people have hurt you as well.

I think humility and vulnerability go hand in hand. We cannot have one without the other, and if I took a survey of all of you reading this, I bet many of you would agree that vulnerability is difficult. It is difficult because vulnerability causes us to feel too exposed, our hearts are too open, and that posture leaves a lot of room for pain and disappointment.

So, when the Bible says in 2 Chronicles 7:14, "If my people, who are called by my name, shall humble themselves, and pray…" I wonder if his instruction was meant for an ongoing posture of humility in our daily lives rather than a singular act done for purposes of prayer.

I have always read that scripture thinking that God was calling us back to a place of prayer and that being humble meant that we bowed a knee to pray. So, I interpreted it like this; "If my people, who are called by my name, would bow their knee and pray…" I never thought that He could actually be calling us to an ongoing posture of humility in our daily lives as we interact with others.

Recently, I had a huge failing event. I was frustrated at myself for my reaction to a situation I felt was unjust.

For the past several years, I have done business with a company that I respect. They were professional, fair, and integral. Last year, the owners sold their business, and it appears the new owners do not share their standard of excellence or value customers as the previous owners had. I received an invoice for services double anything I had ever paid, with an additional charge that was brand new. I was charged for extra time because their calendar differed from the appointment time I had on mine.

Anyone who knows me knows that I live by my calendar. Everything goes on my calendar, so when the technician showed up an hour early, I was frustrated because I had to take time off work to meet them. So, I did not think that the mistake was on my end, and I wrote a lengthy letter to convey the misunderstanding.

Long story short, they didn't care about anything I had to say and were very rude about it. I did not react well. I told them I would not continue my business with them and hung up on them. After hanging up, my first thought was, "How would Brian Guerin have reacted?" (Brian Guerin is the pastor of Ascend Church in Atlanta, Georgia, and he exudes humility.)

I was immediately frustrated with myself.

Recently, I have not been myself, I have been in a season of healing which is code for a season of pain. I know that when God takes us through a healing process, he uses people, places, and things. I have had struggles with people, places, and things in recent months on a whole new level, and I am ashamed to say I haven't always responded in the way that a Christian should (although I have not cussed at them).

I desire to always walk in the fruit of the spirit, but vulnerability and humility are possibly the most difficult postures to master. We all have situations or environments we cannot control. I learned early on that if I didn't like something to just leave and remove people or situations from my life that made me uncomfortable. I spent many years functioning that way. Through that process I learned how to set and keep my own boundaries, but it also left me with very little grace or consideration for others. Everything was all about me, and that kept me safe, free from hurt and judgment and with total control.

But in living that way, I missed the opportunity for God to teach me about humility, grace, and forgiveness. When it comes to people that we love, we don't have the option to walk away, without missing out on opportunities for change and healing, and thus, we are faced with a choice to be prideful, protective or have grace. (Not all situations or people will fit this model, especially where there is active abuse or addiction.)

This is the process of dying to ourselves in order to follow Jesus. It is so much easier to fight than to relent, because we are always protecting our hearts, often through pride, which God hates because it is the exact opposite of humility.

There is so much to say on the subject that I cannot possibly cover everything here. However, I am acutely aware of the areas where pride is ruling my life, and I want that to change. I desire to always respond to situations with grace and humility. I suppose that will be a lifelong endeavor, but I do believe that is what God is asking of all of us.

In the scripture verse mentioned above, there are promises attached. "If my people, who are called by my name, will humble themselves, and pray, and seek my face, and turn from their wicked ways (pride); Then will I hear from heaven, and will forgive their sins, and will heal their land."

In the New Testament, forgiveness was often correlated with healing in the physical body. So when the Bible says He will forgive our sins and heal our land, I believe that is total restoration and redemption. A complete reversal.

I know that we have used this scripture to pray for America, and we should. But in this chapter, I wanted to make it a little more personal and ask us all to check our hearts and allow God to reveal to us the posture of our hearts toward others and toward situations. I cannot say it enough: we must always walk in the place of repentance and surrender.

When I pay the invoice I don't believe I owe, I will write a note of apology. I will swallow my pride and admit that I behaved poorly. That won't be easy, but it is true, and I believe it is what the Lord wants from me.

The prayer for this chapter is powerful, and it can change everything if we pray it from a place of sincerity and endeavor to live it every day! I am going to try. I hope you will as well.

DAY 22

Lord, you said "if my people will humble themselves and pray, then you will forgive us and heal our land. So Lord, we humble ourselves before you and repent for our sins, known sins, and unknown sins. Forgive us Lord and heal our land. We need you to heal our cities, heal our state and heal our nation. In Jesus name!

Declaration

Lord, we declare that as we humbled ourselves to you and walk in humility, that you have forgiven us and you are healing our land, our cities, our state and our nation. In Jesus name.

Chapter Twenty-Three
Rise Up

As I sit down to pen this prayer focus in mid-2024, I think about all the noise going on in the media. It seems like everyone is saying the same thing: "People need to wake up and rise up!" It is true that needs to happen, but at this point, I think we feel we are doing what we can -- or are we? I don't know. I wonder if there is more I can do or should do?

This chapter's prayer is for God to raise up leaders who will bring prayer back to schools. I have pondered many, many times trying to figure out the best way to advocate for prayer to be re-established in our school system. I have written letters to several legal non-profit organizations that specialize in pursuing our constitutional freedoms through the court system, hoping to bring a case that would overturn the Supreme Court ruling of 1962 removing prayer from schools, because I wholeheartedly believe one person can make a difference, as illustrated in the examples below and throughout history. I wrote about this in my book, "Redeem California, With God All Things Are Possible." Below are a few examples of how one person was able to make a difference in a way that changed our religious freedoms and how sports teams observed the American Flag.

In 2000, in Sacramento, California, Michael Newdow brought a legal matter in federal court challenging the "Pledge of Allegiance" on behalf of his elementary school daughter because the pledge says, "One Nation Under God."

I remember being so angry that one person's voice was able to silence the majority in his attempt to take God out of our national pledge, potentially changing how we voiced our allegiance to America. I remember thinking, where are the opposing voices? Why isn't anyone standing up to scream, "No way this can happen!" There were few voices in California opposing him.

I was furious at the wrongness of the situation, but I had no idea how to oppose it. I followed the case, wondering if the atheist would get his way.

This is how it begins. One person stands up for what they believe, and they have the power to affect change.

Look at all the movement former San Francisco 49ers quarterback Colin Kaepernick created when he took a knee during the national anthem at the start of an NFL game in protest of police brutality and racial inequality.

Look at what Madalyn Murray O'Hair, the founder of American Atheists, was able to accomplish as an atheist. Here are a few of her court cases. In each of them, she argued that the separation of church and state had been breached:

- Murray v. Curlett (1963) challenged Bible reading and prayer recitation in Maryland public schools.
- Murray v. United States (1964) to force the Federal Communications Commission to extend the Fairness Doctrine so that atheists could have equal time with religion on radio and television.
- Murray v. Nixon (1970) challenged weekly religious services in the White House.
- O'Hair v. Paine (1971) challenged open readings from the Bible by U.S. astronauts (who are federal employees) during their

spaceflights, spurred by a reading from the book of Genesis by the crew of Apollo 8.

- O'Hair v. Cooke (1977) challenged the opening prayer at city council meetings in Austin, Texas.
- O'Hair v. Blumenthal (1978) challenged the inclusion of the phrase "In God We Trust" on U.S. currency.
- O'Hair v. Hill (1978) to have removed from the Texas Constitution a provision requiring a belief in God of persons holding offices of public trust.
- O'Hair v. Andrus (1979) challenged the use of National Park facilities for the Pope to hold a Roman Catholic mass on the National Mall in Washington, D.C.
- O'Hair v. Clements (1980) tried to remove the Nativity scene displayed in the rotunda of the capitol building in Austin, Texas.
- Carter, et al. v Broadlawns Medical Center, et al. (1984-1987) challenged the full-time employment of an unordained chaplain at a tax-funded county hospital, Broadlawns Medical Center in Des Moines, Iowa.

Her activism led to laws that we live with today. Murray's 1960 lawsuit against the Baltimore City School System was later consolidated with a similar one from Pennsylvania when they reached the U.S. Supreme Court on appeal. The court ruled in 1963 (in Abington School District v. Schempp) that school-sponsored Bible reading in public schools in the United States was unconstitutional. This decision gradually resulted in the end of religious activities sponsored by public schools.

We are living with the actions of people who do not believe in God, yet we not only believe, we understand who He is and what He is capable of doing. He is God over all things!

While the Supreme Court cases will stand, I think there were liberties taken that did not need to be taken. In other words, I think schools interrupted the ruling differently back then, and there is room for reconsideration by the court, namely, "school-sponsored." I believe we can get prayers back in schools as long as they are voluntary, and the districts do not mandate them. We need someone to challenge that previous ruling and bring the topic back to the forefront of conversation. Perhaps then, we may see a decrease in school-aged suicides.

Change is happening across the United States. The Governors of Louisiana and Alabama just instituted new laws mandating the Ten Commandments be posted in every classroom and prohibiting DEI/Diversity, Equity, Inclusion initiatives in the classrooms. This is a huge move in the right direction.

What do you think it will take for California to turn? Newly elected officials? More people voting? More people waking up? Yes, all of the above. But like I said a few chapters ago, I want back what the enemy has stolen from us! I want California to be great again. It is the most majestic state in the union.

I believe that our prayers are making a difference, and God is moving on behalf of our prayers.

I believe California needs people who will rise up and run for elected office and govern in the fear of the Lord. The problem is that there is a shortage of candidates who can win an election. Will you help me pray that God would raise up leaders to lead California back to a place of morality and integrity and raise up those who would fight to see prayer return to the classroom?

I believe we are going to see it happen because it is needed now more than ever. So, let's band together, pray, and watch what God will do!

DAY 23

Lord, we ask that you raise up leaders in our state government that will reinstate the right to pray in schools. We ask that every right that has been taken from Christians be reinstituted through new leadership in California In Jesus name!

Declaration

Lord, we declare that prayer will return to our schools in California and across the nation. In Jesus name.

Chapter Twenty-Four
The Powers that Be

In 1994 and 1995, I had the privilege of working for the Visalia Police Department. I started as a volunteer and was later hired, working in several departments wherever I was needed. I had a unique advantage as a volunteer because I had access to many departments of the agency. During my time there I went on many ride-alongs, mostly with the gang unit. I had a front-row seat observing the streets of my community and the men and women who served to keep us safe.

One night while I was out with the gang unit, we received a request for backup on a felony stop in progress. The officer I was with rolled code three (a request for priority response), in order to receive additional back-up as soon as possible. I didn't know what a felony stop was at the time; I just knew it was serious. A felony stop is very intense and dangerous for all involved and there is a possibility of the use of force by the police. They are rarer and more intrusive than regular traffic stops. Felony stops occur when the police see a vehicle that has been reported stolen, or the vehicle has been used in a crime, or there is a warrant for the registered owner of the vehicle. This night, the car was reported stolen.

As we arrived on the scene, the vehicle was in the middle of an intersection, surrounded on all four sides by law enforcement. Officers were out of the patrol car, behind the car doors, guns drawn, ordering the occupants of the vehicle to exit the car with their hands up.

I was not allowed to get out of the car. I watched with bated breath as these men, whom I knew personally, quickly found themselves in danger. I distinctly remember looking over at one of them and seeing the nervousness on his face. I felt his discomfort from where I was. I can still see it today. Thankfully, that night ended with a couple of arrests, and everyone went home safely to their families.

That was not the case in 1998 when one of our officers was shot and killed in the line of duty. That morning the SWAT team executed a search warrant, and he was the first one to breach the door. Officer James Rapozo was 33 years old at the time, with a wife and two young children. Our department had not had an officer killed in the line of duty since 1946. In 1998, they had their second.

Although I had moved on from the department by then, I kept in touch with the friends I had established there and returned home to attend the funeral. Although I have attended many funerals in my life, I had never attended a funeral for a fallen police officer. It was incredibly moving and gave me a new understanding of the brotherhood that exists among the law enforcement community. There was an honor that I had not experienced before, and it was beautiful to witness and be part of.

Later, in the course of my profession as a marriage and family therapist, I had the privilege to work with several first responders for various reasons. One had been shot three times while chasing a suspect. He knew that God had kept him alive, as one bullet hit the dead center of the chest and he was only saved by his ballistic vest. The other two bullets penetrated muscle in two places but missed the arteries. This person was so humble and just happy to be alive. Almost all the officers I have ever met have been men and women of integrity. I honor our law enforcement community and am thankful that, despite the difficulties, they still wish to serve.

GOD OF THE IMPOSSIBLE!

Law enforcement officers have been under tremendous scrutiny in recent years with a rise in accusations of racial violence, police brutality, and wrongful death suits. It is hard to know what is true these days with so many deep fake videos, propaganda, and the overall lawlessness taking place in California and across our nation. California has all but tied the hands of law enforcement, and the courts have little authority to hold anyone accountable.

In addition to those accusations, there is an alarming rise of violence against our law enforcement officers, unseen in our history. In 2023, there were 79,091 assaults against law enforcement officers in the United States, marking the highest rate of officer assaults in the past decade. The majority of these assaults occurred while officers were responding to simple assaults (6,783 incidents) and drug/narcotic violations (4,879 incidents). Additionally, the number of officers assaulted and injured by firearms reached a ten-year high, with approximately 466 officers affected.

One of the reasons I wanted to specifically pray over our officers is because not only do they keep us and our community safe, but they are literally the instruments of God. The Bible says in Romans 13:1-6,

"Let every soul be subject unto the higher powers. For there is no power but of God: the powers that be are ordained of God. Whosoever therefore resisteth the power, the ordinance of God: and they that resist shall receive to themselves damnation. For rulers are not a terror to good works, but to the evil. Wilt thou then not be afraid of the power? do that which is good, and thou shalt have praise of the same: For he is the minister of God to thee for good. But if thou do that which is evil, be afraid; for he beareth not the sword in vain: for he is the minister of God, a revenger to execute wrath upon him that doeth evil. Wherefore ye must needs be subject, not only for wrath, but also for conscience sake. For this cause pay ye tribute also: for they are God's ministers, attending continually upon this very thing" (NKJV).

So right now, will you join me in praying this prayer over our law enforcement community? Who knows what lives will be saved as a result of our prayers.

DAY 24

Lord, we pray against every act of violence, false accusation and malicious intent that would cause harm to our law enforcement community across the state of California. We ask that you increase integrity to all law enforcement officers and restore their badge of honor that has been tarnished by those who seek division. In Jesus name!

Declaration

Lord, we declare that the spirit of accusation and violence perpetrated against our law enforcement community will cease and integrity and honor is now returning to position each officer holds. In Jesus name.

Chapter Twenty-Five
Healing from Self-Condemnation

Guilt and self-condemnation are difficult emotions that trap us in cycles of depression, anxiety, and dysfunctional behavior that only perpetuate the confirmation bias, that there is something wrong with us, or that we are somehow not good enough.

As I have shared throughout the course of this book, I have been on my own healing journey for about the past 10 years. Most of the things I have needed healing from have been from things done to me, injustices I suffered, and the realization of how hurt I felt as a young girl. As children, we just accept things as they are, because on some level, we understand our own helplessness. I believe the foundation of healing that I have already gone through prior to this, was necessary for this latest layer of healing that God is walking me through and hopefully walking my loved ones through.

That layer has to do with the hurt I caused to others. You have probably heard the saying, "hurt people hurt other people," it is very true, whether we mean to cause harm or not. I certainly never meant to cause harm to those that I loved, but I did out of my own selfish needs driven by survival instincts. It's not an excuse, just a reality.

Sometimes I wonder if God allowed me to become a therapist, knowing I would need the knowledge to process my own experiences in life someday.

Although I never wrestled with anxiety or depression, I did become a workaholic, a perfectionist, and unhealthily independent. It wasn't until I had a conversation with my son a few years back that I realized I was still living in a survival mentality. Those traits served me well for much of my life until the Lord began to show me what they were masking. Those behaviors masked the deep root of rejection, and the feeling of never being good enough for anyone. I was completely oblivious to that, though. The Lord's great love and kindness for me, began to reveal the ways in which I was masking my fear, and slowly changed those things.

Over the past three or so years, the deepest and very old wound began to surface. The depth of pain I had experienced long ago, had been buried for many years. As it has surfaced it has cut to the depth of my soul, and is beginning to have serious ramifications and consequences for me now. I am remembering things for the first time after 30+ years, memories that have been buried deep down in my soul that never went away and never healed. I am again experiencing regret and realizations, that I had buried to survive the loss. It is painful to know that I can never change what caused harm to someone I would give my life for.

Someday, when the situation is resolved, I will write about it, but I am still knee-deep in the middle of the exposing and healing process. I have spent hours over the years mourning, trying to be better, trying to make it up in ways I could, asking God for forgiveness, asking the people involved for forgiveness, regretting, and wishing I had known a different way. But I, like many of you, cannot change the past. My actions profoundly affected others in ways I can never take back. Only God can heal a heart. I know that. I believe that. I am thankful for that. But we still have to live out the experiences of pain, sorrow and regret.

GOD OF THE IMPOSSIBLE!

Over the last two years, I have been in a wrestling match with my thoughts, my emotions, my love in this situation, my need to self-protect, my knowledge of how God works in the heart of people, my desire to walk in obedience to the Lord and my own willingness to die to my flesh. In this case, guilt, fear and pride. It's been grueling, and I have had some failures, but I think I am in a better place now with myself and the Lord, which is why I can write about guilt and self-condemnation.

When the battle is raging, and the fire of purification is intense, we cannot always see clearly, and it is easy to fear, lose faith, and worry that people and situations will never change. The enemy whispers in our ears, "History is repeating itself," "This is the way it's always going to be," "you will never…." and a variety of other messages that bring intense fear, sorrow, and doubt.

But I am here to testify that God is a redeemer and a restorer, and the devil is a liar! Though my circumstances are incredibly painful, and sorrow exists, I no longer allow the enemy to condemn me for things I cannot change and for things that God has forgiven me for. But beyond that, I know, that I know, that I know, God makes ALL things good, and He uses everything in our life for good if we allow him to.

Through this experience, I am learning how to become better at expressing vulnerability. It is hard for me, especially because the people I am dealing with have a very low opinion of me, and my vulnerability feels like it gets trampled on, but I am showing up the best I know how at this time and accepting the things I cannot control. I know that as I heal, I will get better at expressing vulnerability.

I have already overcome a lot in my life and have done a lot of work to ensure a better future by completely surrendering to the Lord and His process. I had no idea this situation would ever or could ever happen at this point in life, but it is here. It has come as a complete shock to me, but

I know it is necessary for true healing to take place for all. It feels like God saved the hardest wound for last, but I believe it is because it will bring the greatest blessing and an abundance of love and restoration that has been missing most all my life. He is holding my heart and their heart, in his hands and I take great comfort in that.

If there is any area of your life that you cannot let go of or forgive yourself for, I encourage you to ask God to help you be willing to explore that with Him. We must be willing to allow him to work and uproot what has been buried. Many people are unwilling because they fear the pain of exposure and the helplessness of addressing old wounds. However, I can promise that if you give God permission and access to your heart, you will never regret it. Though it will be painful emotionally, redemption and restoration are possible, and your healing is ALWAYS the result.

Forgive others, forgive yourself, be grateful every day and "lean not unto your own understanding, but in all your ways acknowledge Him, and He will direct your path" (Prov. 3:5-6)

Pray this prayer with me and text it to others who need to forgive themselves.

DAY 25

Lord, there are many who do not forgive themselves for things they have done. Please deal with their heart and let them feel your love for them so they will believe forgiveness is possible. Bring them to the place where they can and will forgive themselves. In Jesus name!

Declaration

Lord, we declare that the love of Jesus will fall on those who feel unloved, and through his love, they will love themselves and receive His forgiveness. In Jesus name.

Chapter Twenty-Six
From Apathy to Passion

I was at a gathering over the weekend and conversed with a high school math teacher. He loves his job and has been teaching for over 30 years. He conveyed deep discouragement about the way kids treat their education in today's society compared to just 10 years ago. He said it is difficult to engage them, and they do not interact in the classroom very much, if at all. The change has affected him to the point he is looking to change careers.

On the other end of the education spectrum, I have a friend who is a preschool teacher in one of our poorest and most challenging districts. She reports that the kids need a lot of resources, in addition to needing much more attention, engagement, and praise. The kids need more because they are lacking it at home. They are also younger, innocent and sometimes underdeveloped, mentally and emotionally.

My caseload is about 50% school-aged kids. I have had the pleasure of working with some amazing school counselors and principals. When school personnel invest in the students and care for them, it can literally be life-saving.

Sadly, I have met other teachers and school staff who are not invested at all. Perhaps they are overwhelmed by the need in our school system, or perhaps they have just grown apathetic.

Schools are our first line of defense after the family, and if the family environment is problematic, then schools are the first to evaluate the needs and well-being of a child. All school personnel are mandated reporters who are required to report suspected child abuse or neglect. Based on my caseload, I can tell you that many school personnel are not reporting. I imagine it is because they have done so in the past, and nothing ever happens. I imagine they feel like it wouldn't matter anyway; the kiddo will be sent back to their home, as many of them are. I get it. I think we all have felt like our voice isn't enough to make a difference at some point or another.

If you are someone who works in the school setting reading this, and you have taken the time to report incidents of suspected child abuse or neglect, thank you! If you have not reported, we need you to.

I am not a fan of the child welfare system. We need a ton of reform in this area. I have written on this in the past. However, they have been very instrumental in getting kids to safety in severe cases, and I am grateful for that. For now, they are the system that is in place to provide assistance. Although 95% of cases are not investigated, we must still do our part and use our voice. Statistics for the 95%?

When I wrote "Redeem California, With God All Things Are Possible," it was to inspire faith, to inspire passion, and most importantly, to remind us all, that God is the difference maker in all the things that are wrong with California and the nation. I, too, had grown very apathetic in my involvement and using the voice God gave me , even struggling with hope for my own future. After Covid, I was discouraged and had to get a new perspective from heaven. That change of perspective was two-fold.

First, God reminded me who He was and who I was not! He is the one who sits on the throne, who has power over all things, on earth, under the earth, and in the heavenly places. He has all power over everything;

absolutely everything answers to Him. He reminded me that I am ONLY a vessel. It isn't about my accomplishments or failures, but it's about being a vessel through which He can work. I knew that somewhere inside my head, but when I was divinely reminded, I let go of everything I had hoped for and aligned myself with the knowledge that whatever comes next will be because of God's divine purpose.

Second, I felt the Lord whisper, "What is in your hands? Occupy until I come!" At the time that this word came, we were on lockdown. I was going to work and seeing clients, but there was little else to do. My voice was what I had. Ironically, my voice is also what He uses in my work. I talk and listen for a living. So, I began writing more. I began speaking up more, hoping to illuminate what was happening in California and globally. The book came not long after that.

My book hasn't sold very much to date, but I didn't write it to make money. I wrote it to encourage people not to give up and to remind them of who God is and who we are in Him. We are not helpless. My voice and what I could do with it was in my hands. That was all I knew to do.

It is easy to become discouraged. It is easy to do nothing. It is easy to blend into the crowd and not draw attention to oneself. But what has God given to you to be used for His kingdom? Where has He placed you? Wherever you are, that is your mission field.

Although the prayer for this chapter is for our school staff, I pray that all of us will engage in life more and use the voice He has given to each of us to show up in situations, speak the truth in love, regardless of the price, and do what is right in all situations, regardless of if we think it makes a difference. Our job is to do our part. God is the only one who can control the outcome.

We desperately need our school personnel to find their passion again, fight for the kids again, speak truth to power, and reach out to the kids they observe who might need help. We cannot be afraid of the outcome. We cannot be apathetic. We must use what is in our hands and occupy ourselves until He comes.

DAY 26

Lord, I pray for every teacher, school counselor, and all school staff across the state of California. Empower them to speak up if they see a child being abused, mistreated, neglected, bullied, or falling behind. Give them increased awareness so that they may protect our children entrusted to their care. In Jesus name!

Declaration

Lord, we declare that teachers, counselors, and all school staff will be empowered to speak the truth into intervene in situations in order to protect children. In Jesus name.

Chapter Twenty-Seven
Walking in Divine Order

I have observed a growing dynamic among men and women in relationships. The way relationships function in today's society is exactly backward to the divine order in which they were meant to function. It is no surprise to me that there is such a high divorce rate and a high prevalence of infidelity and pornography addiction among both genders. We have a society of women who dominate their husbands and men who let them. There is also a high prevalence of men who do not work and allow the woman to be the sole provider. It is exactly the opposite of the natural role of each gender (of course, there are always exceptions). It doesn't work for very long, and those who function in these dynamics are often left unfulfilled.

I do not say these things out of judgment. I was guilty of such relationships myself. None of my relationships worked, no matter how committed and how hard I tried they all ended badly. I say this because people everywhere are looking for meaningful relationships filled with love and connection, and there is a way that does, in fact, work. I want people to have meaningful and fulfilling relationships the way God designed us to have them, with true intimacy, true connection, and true oneness.

The Bible says in Proverbs 14:12, "There is a way that seems right to man, but the end thereof is death." Scripture is both literal and metaphorical. In this passage, death can mean a number of things: the death of a dream, the death of an idea, the death of hope, the death of innocence, and the death of trust. You get the picture.

Many times, when I am counseling someone after a breakup or a divorce, the loss they are struggling with the most is the loss of what they hoped the relationship would have been. Yet, repeatedly, they repeat the same familiar patterns and attract the same familiar mate, ending with the same dysfunctional relationship.

We are a culture that wants things now, instant gratification, which is the opposite of the biblical fruit of the spirit, patience. Rarely are people willing to be patient when getting to know someone. They meet, they have sex, they move in together, and then expect happily ever after. Seldom does that ever work. I admit, there are some occasions when it does, but it is rare. The reason is that the relationship was established out of order, lacking some fundamental ingredients for strong, lasting, loving relationships.

I have a friend who says, "Do it God's way and get God's results." I have come to adopt that phrase myself, not because it sounds Christianly, even though it is, but because it is absolutely true. I have learned throughout my life that God's ways are perfect, and they always end in fruitfulness and inner fulfillment. I have tested the theory, and it is true. I will spend my life pursuing the Lord and obeying His word. He is the embodiment of Love. He knew what He was doing when He designed how couples should function. It was out of His immense love for us that he gave us the blueprint so that we could walk in the God-ordained love that He created us to have. The entire Bible is a book about the love of a husband for a wife. Of course, it is much more than that, but God is pursuing his bride throughout the Bible, painting a picture of what unconditional love and forgiveness looks like. There is a right and wrong way to be in a relationship with God, and the right way flows 100% through love.

This may be a little too traditional for some of you, but there is a reason traditional relationships work. I tried it every way possible, thinking I could circumvent the hard work. One has to ask themselves: How much is it worth to have a right, lasting, loving relationship built on the right foundation? What price am I willing to pay? Anything of value takes time, patience, and perseverance. God does not make mistakes. His formula works.

Not long ago, I had the pleasure of attending the most beautiful wedding I have ever witnessed. Although the groom was handsome, the bride was gorgeous, and the décor was classic, that was not the reason the wedding made such an impression on me.

It made an impression on me because the bride and the groom had kept themselves for marriage due to their love and commitment to the Lord. There was a purity I could feel that transcended the physical. Everything about the wedding was honoring to one another and to God. As I was listening to the minister talk about each of them, I was overcome with emotion and revelation. As I became aware of the innocence they were giving to each other, a tapestry began to form in my mind, and suddenly, I could see the enormous benefits of doing marriage God's way. They purely trusted each other and desired a committed and consecrated life together, and there were no barriers between them, so they could give themselves to each other fully.

They would not have to worry about insecurity because trust existed. They would not have to worry about jealousy because love existed. They would not have to worry about porn or infidelity because they had kept themselves pure. There was no question on who would lead the union; in strength, love, and commitment to God, he would. He was honored to. She was honored to be the woman and let him lead. She was honored to be his adorning spouse. She was her own person, secure in her position.

She was honored to walk beside him and face life together as one. It was a beautiful sight to behold.

But I wept for multiple reasons throughout the ceremony and wept for three hours after, as I made the drive home.

I was flooded with emotions as the film of my life continued to play before me in high definition. Although I had already been through much healing, this area held much sorrow. At the same time, I could clearly see the love God has for me and for all of us. He only wants the best for our lives if we can trust and believe that.

Obedience is not a rule we must follow; it is a choice. It is not a list of what I have to do or cannot do; it is a choice. Obedience comes as a result of love. I wasn't taught that growing up. I was taught that if I followed the rules, I would be saved, and if I sinned according to the rules, I was going to hell. As a young person, love was not part of the equation as far as I could understand. The emphasis was on the rules. I don't fault anyone for that; everyone does their best with what they know, and I am grateful for being raised in a home that taught me about Jesus.

I had known that obedience came from love for some time, but on the day of this wedding, witnessing what felt like a holy union allowed me to have a much deeper understanding of why God's way is the best way, not for selfish gain but because it is the truest form of love, trust, and intimacy.

I know the wedding I described above is incredibly rare in our culture, but they do exist. None of us can change our past. Whatever our past has been, God has forgiven us. It is never too late to become the man or woman, husband or wife you were meant to be. It will cost you something, but I promise it will be worth the price.

In this process, God is individually refining us and purifying us. Relationships are always meant to reflect our relationship with the Lord and the kind of relationship He wants to have with us. In the Bible, men are reflected as the groom and women as the bride. In this, our roles are clearly defined, but it is not that simple to live out. I heard a pastor once say, "Every simplicity begins as a complexity." Relationships are incredibly complex, but if we stay in God's order, we will get His results.

Whatever relationship you find yourself in today, know that God has already been in your future, and he knows how to lead you if you trust Him. Please pray this with me today for all men and women.

Lord, we ask that you raise up men who will be strong men and women who will be women in roles you ordained, for your ways are perfect. Remove the fear from men and replace it with love to lead and serve their families. In Jesus name!

Declaration

Lord, we declare that men and women will return to their God-ordained roles in the family. In Jesus name.

GOD OF THE IMPOSSIBLE!

Chapter Twenty-Eight
Holy Reverence

What does it mean when Christians say, "God is Holy," or when we talk about the "fear of the Lord?" What does Holy reverence mean? How do we live this out? These concepts are difficult to grasp, as they require revelation and come only through experience with God.

When I was young, I routinely had nightmares and was deathly afraid of the dark. I felt there was something watching me at night while trying to sleep. I had several sleep paralysis events and once woke up to see three demons surrounding my bed. The dark felt alive to me, and it wasn't until I was 28 years old that I could sleep with all the lights off and not be afraid.

That is what fear looks like to me. I had very real experiences with what I considered to be evil manifestations. I had a respect for the darkness that caused me to avoid it.

When I began reading my Bible at age 28, I remember reading passages that said "…and he was sore afraid," and that usually occurred when the angel of the Lord showed up to give a word to someone. I used to think to myself, why would the presence of the angel of the Lord cause someone to feel "sore afraid?" I didn't understand for the longest time until I had my own encounter with the reverential fear of the Lord.

The fear of the Lord is an experience with His existence that causes one to understand, in some small way, the enormity of how powerful, mighty, and Holy, God really is. It is often life-changing in a good way.

The Bible gives us several examples of people who experienced God in a way that gave them a new reverence and fear of Him. One is found in Daniel 5:1-9: I did not proof the verses as I assumed you'd copied them directly.

"Belshazzar the king made a great feast to a thousand of his lords and drank wine before the thousand. Belshazzar, while he tasted the wine, commanded to bring the golden and silver vessels which his father Nebuchadnezzar had taken out of the temple which was in Jerusalem; that the king, and his princes, his wives, and his concubines, might drink therein. Then they brought the golden vessels that were taken out of the temple of the house of God which was at Jerusalem; and the king, and his princes, his wives, and his concubines, drank in them. They drank wine, and praised the gods of gold, and of silver, of brass, of iron, of wood, and of stone. In the same hour came forth fingers of a man's hand and wrote over against the candlestick upon the plaster of the wall of the king's palace: and the king saw the part of the hand that wrote. Then the king's countenance was changed, and his thoughts troubled him, so that the joints of his loins were loosed, and his knees smote one against another. The king cried aloud to bring in the astrologers, the Chaldeans, and the soothsayers. And the king spoke, and said to the wise men of Babylon, Whosoever shall read this writing, and shew me the interpretation thereof, shall be clothed with scarlet, and have a chain of gold about his neck, and shall be the third ruler in the kingdom. Then came in all the king's wise men: but they could not read the writing, nor make known to the king the interpretation thereof. Then was king Belshazzar greatly troubled, and his countenance was changed in him, and his lords were astonished."

Another instance is found in the story of Balaam. In Numbers 22:1-35:

"And the children of Israel set forward and pitched in the plains of Moab on this side Jordan by Jericho. And Balak the son of Zippor saw all that Israel had done to the Amorites. And Moab was sore afraid of the people, because they were many: and Moab was distressed because of the children of Israel. And Moab said unto the elders of Midian, now shall this company lick up all that are round about us, as the ox licketh up the grass of the field. And Balak the son of Zippor was king of the Moabites at that time. He sent messengers therefore unto Balaam the son of Beor to Pethor, which is by the river of the land of the children of his people, to call him, saying, Behold, there is a people come out from Egypt: behold, they cover the face of the earth, and they abide over against me: Come now therefore, I pray thee, curse me this people; for they are too mighty for me: peradventure I shall prevail, that we may smite them, and that I may drive them out of the land: for I wot that he whom thou blessest is blessed, and he whom thou cursest is cursed. And the elders of Moab and the elders of Midian departed with the rewards of divination in their hand; and they came unto Balaam, and spake unto him the words of Balak. And he said unto them, Lodge here this night, and I will bring you word again, as the LORD shall speak unto me: and the princes of Moab abode with Balaam. And God came unto Balaam, and said, what men are these with thee? And Balaam said unto God, Balak the son of Zippor, king of Moab, hath sent unto me, saying, behold, there is a people come out of Egypt, which covereth the face of the earth: come now, curse me them; peradventure I shall be able to overcome them, and drive them out. And God said unto Balaam, thou shalt not go with them; thou shalt not curse the people: for they are blessed. And Balaam rose up in the morning, and said unto the princes of Balak, get you into your land: for the LORD refuseth to give me leave to go with you. And the princes of Moab rose up, and they went unto Balak, and said, Balaam refuseth to come with us. And Balak sent yet again princes, more, and more honourable than they. And they came to Balaam, and said to him, Thus saith Balak the son of Zippor, Let nothing, I pray thee, hinder thee from coming unto me: For I will promote thee unto very great honour, and I will do whatsoever thou sayest unto me: come therefore, I pray thee, curse me this people. And Balaam answered and said unto the servants of Balak, If Balak would give me his house full of silver and gold, I cannot go beyond the word of the LORD my God, to do less or more. Now therefore, I pray you, tarry ye also here this night, that I may know what the LORD will say unto me more. And God came unto Balaam at night, and said unto him, If the men come to call thee, rise up, and go with them; but yet the word which I shall say unto thee, that shalt thou do. And Balaam rose up in the morning, and saddled his ass, and went with the princes of Moab. And God's anger was kindled because he went: and the angel of the LORD stood in the way for an adversary against him. Now he was riding upon his ass, and his two servants were with him. And the ass saw the angel of the LORD standing in the way, and his sword drawn in his hand: and the ass turned aside out of the way and went into the field: and Balaam smote the ass, to turn her into the way. But the angel of the LORD stood in a path of the vineyards, a wall being on this side, and a wall on that side. And when the ass saw the angel of the LORD, she thrust herself unto the wall, and crushed Balaam's foot against the wall: and he smote her again. And the angel of the LORD went further, and stood in a narrow place, where was no way to turn either to the right hand or to the left. And when the ass saw the angel of the LORD, she fell down under Balaam: and Balaam's anger was kindled, and he smote the ass with a staff. And the LORD opened the mouth of the ass, and she said unto Balaam, what have I done unto thee, that thou hast smitten me these three times? And Balaam said unto the ass, because thou hast mocked me: I would there were a sword in mine hand, for now would I kill thee. And the ass said unto Balaam, am not I thine ass, upon which thou hast ridden ever since I was thine unto this day? was I ever wont to do so unto thee? And he said, Nay. Then the LORD opened the eyes of Balaam, and he saw the angel of the LORD standing in the way, and his sword drawn in his hand: and he bowed down his head and fell flat on his face. And the angel of the LORD said unto him, Wherefore hast thou smitten thine ass these three times? behold, I went out to withstand thee, because thy way is perverse before me: And the ass saw me, and turned from me these three times: unless she had turned from me, surely now also I had slain thee, and saved her alive. And Balaam said unto the angel of the LORD, I have sinned; for I knew not that thou stood in the way against me: now therefore, if it displease thee, I will get me back again. And the angel of the LORD said unto Balaam, go with the men: but only the word that I shall speak unto thee, that thou shalt speak."

In both cases, God showed up to get their attention and caused them to understand their own frailty in comparison to Him.

There have been a handful of times that I have experienced the presence of God in a powerful way that caused me to glimpse his power in a reverential way. It is difficult to convey with words, as words are not sufficient to describe the overall experience and revelation that occurred.

The closest thing I can use to describe what I felt at those times, is when I hear thunder. Thunder immediately reminds me of just how big and powerful God is, in the way my limited mind understands, as if that is His voice sounding throughout the earth. It is the best example that I can come up with to express what the fear of the Lord feels like and the reverence it demands.

The world is spiraling so quickly toward total depravity. We are witnessing the beginning of Christian persecution and a Godless society. The only thing that will change the trajectory of the world is for God to make his existence known and felt by all. We need a sovereign move of God that will bring the fear of the Lord upon the earth. An encounter that cannot be denied or ignored. Those living in blatant sexual perversion, lawlessness, and disdain for anything holy are ignorant of the existence of a Holy God. Either they don't believe He exists, or they don't believe He has any power, or they don't believe that He takes an interest in what humans do on the earth. They couldn't be more wrong. The only way they will come to understand those truths is if God reveals himself to them in an undeniable and personal way. He does this for us because of His great mercy and love for us.

In both stories I shared from the Bible, each were done to correct a wrong and to give an opportunity for the people to repent and change what they were doing. This prayer is a request for God to move in such a way on all who hold public office and upon the people in California that they will understand the fear of the Lord and His holiness enough to change the way they lead and govern. We need God to step into the affairs of California and the United States, and sovereignty must move in an undeniable way.

Pray this with me and watch what God will do!

Lord, we ask that you release divine fear of the Lord upon the people in our cities throughout California. We ask that you release a divine fear of the Lord upon all those in public office throughout California. Let there be a Holy Reverence for you. In Jesus Name!

Declaration

Lord, we declare that the fear of the Lord will return to the people of California, and that our nation would understand their need for a savior. In Jesus name.

GOD OF THE IMPOSSIBLE!

Chapter Twenty-Nine
The Reality of Hell

Hell is a topic few of us want to discuss. It is controversial in some Christian circles, especially after Rob Bell's book, *Love Wins*, hit the market in 2012. An entire new doctrine surfaced, one that promotes hell as something we suffer on earth instead of an eternal lake fire described in the Bible, where there will be unending darkness, torment, and separation from God. Complete aloneness. I don't think any of us can fathom that.

Many years ago, when I was in my early twenties, I was out one night with friends. Towards the end of the evening, a fight broke out in front of me, and a young man was beaten to the point of unconsciousness. I had never witnessed brutality being inflicted on a complete stranger with such rage.

I did not stand by and watch. I jumped in and tried to stop it with many others until the police and ambulance arrived. I did not know any of the parties involved and did not know the reason for the fight. All I knew was that a guy was pulverized by a group of people until he was unresponsive and bleeding from all areas of the face.

I was so scared for him and felt so helpless. I thought about that guy for weeks, months, and years after. I was so sad for him and wondered many times over the years how he dealt with such trauma after getting out of the hospital.

Mob violence has become a thing now; it is increasingly common. I wonder how many of us are becoming desensitized to it. Desensitized to the riots, the school shootings, the drug overdoses, and the fatalities that occur every day for one reason or another?

According to the World Death Clock, approximately 106 people die every minute in the world. I cannot comprehend that. But I do look at the newspaper obituaries daily, aware that someone's family member is no longer on this earth but in eternity somewhere.

The older I get, the more aware I am of how little time I have left. I think about all the work that still needs to be done to reach people with the message of the cross. For every person I come across and can encourage, there are hundreds more who need help. There are so many who need to be seen, heard, and cared for. How are we going to reach these people?

I pray that our hearts will not become calloused by all the depravity around us and that we continue to have compassion for individuals. Watching someone almost get beaten to death was awful, and my heart broke for him, but it does not compare to what it would feel like if someone I care for missed heaven.

Hell is a real place that was created for Satan and his angels. However, the Bible is clear, that those who do not chose to serve the Lord will also end up there by default of their choices. I do not want to see anyone end up there. It feels to me that there is not enough time to reach the lost, so I pray Luke 4:18. The Spirit of the Lord is upon me, because he hath anointed me to preach the gospel to the poor; he hath sent me to heal the brokenhearted, to preach deliverance to the captives, and recovering of sight to the blind, to set at liberty them that are bruised I know that God can reach them and draw them unto himself.

I believe the day is coming soon when people will be returning to the house of God. Those who have never been to church will go to church to look for hope. Those who have turned away from God will return to Him, seeking answers for their weary souls. Those who have only heard stories of Jesus will go to church to see if what they heard is true. When this happens, we must be ready to receive them. We must be ready to have our routine disrupted, and we must be ready to see people through the eyes of love, the way that Jesus sees them, because eternity is real, and all of us are going to either heaven or hell.

This chapter's prayer is for pastors. I pray that the Lord will increase their burden for the lost and that their faith will be strengthened, and I pray they will know God will do the impossible through them, through us, and all who trust in Him to reach the lost for Jesus.

DAY 29

Lord, we ask that you give pastors, across California, a burden for the lost. Remind them that you are the God of the impossible. Strengthen their faith to believe that nothing is too hard for you. Let them declare the truth that you have given us power and authority to defeat our enemy. In Jesus name!

Declaration

Lord we declare that pastors across our State and Nation will have an extra measure of faith to see the loss saved in record numbers. In Jesus name.

GOD OF THE IMPOSSIBLE!

Chapter Thirty
Removing that Which Causes Harm

There is a very old mantra that use to be passed down in families, Sunday schools and institutions. It is commonly referred to as "the golden rule" and it has worked for generations. Its origin can be traced to various religious and philosophical traditions but is most famously articulated from the passage in the Bible found in Matthew 7:12 "do unto others as you would have them do unto you."

This principle of reciprocity and ethical conduct is not unique to Christianity. Other cultures and religions, such as Judaism, Islam, Confucianism and Hinduism, also believe when the Golden Rule is applied, it transcends individual religious and cultural boundaries, emphasizing empathy and mutual respect. Applying this principle in our individual lives leaves little room for hate, division and judgement.

As an aside, there is a huge misconception between the left and the right and Christians are blamed for hating groups of people that live differently then they do. However, I would propose that Christians do not hate groups of people. They merely do not want to be forced to accept things that they do not believe in and there is a difference. There has been a reverse discrimination agenda targeting Christians and very much misrepresenting them in regard to differing moral and value-based beliefs. Real Christians do live by the Golden Rule and have no problem allowing people to make their own choices, so long as those choices do not legislate against our personal and individual rights under the constitution. That is when it becomes the problem we are seeing today. There has been an infringement, an overstepping of boundaries, that has occurred politically and as a result has misrepresented and misconstrued the heart of Christ followers.

When individual values and morality is compromised, society as a whole begins to decline, we have experienced since the 1960's and the advent of "do what makes you feel good." We stopped being a collective and became individualized, which resulted in the social construct of today. Corruption, lawlessness, dishonesty and abuse of power is not only the norm in some circles, but it is somewhat expected. Could our societal issues be solved if we lived by the Golden Rule?

In the healthcare sector, doctors take the Hippocratic Oath to "do no harm." There is a societal assumption that doctors are good and trustworthy. Likewise, the law enforcement community also take an oath of office to "serve and protect" when they are sworn in for duty, and the majority of them take it very seriously.

Unfortunately, like any sector we have discussed throughout this book, there are those who do not abide by ethical and moral conduct and cause the reputation of the whole to become tainted.

Corruption is quickly becoming a bigger concern then what it has been in years past. Corruption can arise from various factors, often intertwined with systemic, environmental, and individual influences. Here are some common causes:

- Organizational Culture: A culture that tolerates or even promotes unethical behavior can lead to corruption. If senior officers are corrupt or ignore misconduct, this behavior can trickle down to the rank and file.

- Lack of Accountability: When there is insufficient oversight or weak disciplinary measures, officers may feel they can act with impunity. Effective internal affairs departments and external review boards are essential in maintaining accountability.
- Low Pay and Poor Working Conditions: In some regions, low salaries and inadequate working conditions can drive officers to seek supplementary income through corrupt means.
- Opportunity: High levels of discretion and access to illicit markets can provide ample opportunities for corruption. This includes bribery, theft, and involvement in organized crime.
- Peer Pressure and Solidarity: The "blue wall of silence" or strong sense of loyalty among officers can discourage whistleblowing and encourage cover-ups of corrupt activities.
- Personal Greed and Ambition: Individual factors such as personal greed, ambition, and a lack of ethical grounding can also lead to corrupt behavior.
- Exposure to Criminal Elements: Regular interaction with criminals can sometimes result in officers becoming involved in illegal activities themselves, either through coercion or temptation.

The greater good of how society functions, and humanity as a whole, depends on our individual ethics and morality, hence the Golden Rule. Our choices, including how we vote and how we pray are also a determining factor. We need to pray for all the people we place in positions of power and authority that they will serve with honor, strength, dignity and morality. We also need to pray for those who are corrupt, dishonest, immoral and unethical, that they would be removed.

We have prayed a similar prayer specifically for others in authority, but this prayer is for the law enforcement community. In a world where good and evil exists, we pray that good prevails.

DAY 30

Lord, as with all our elected officials and those in leadership, we ask that you remove any law enforcement officer from their position if they are corrupt, dishonest, or abusive in any way. Replace them with men and women of honor who seek to serve. In Jesus name!

Declaration

Lord, we declare that God will raise up new law enforcement officers who are honorable and who seek to serve the people of California and our nation in righteousness and in truth. In Jesus name.

One Final Thought

When writing this book, I pondered how much personal information to share and the style of writing I wanted to bring to this project. I had written these chapters over the course of 30 weeks, beginning in January and ending in August 2024.

I have always believed in truth and transparency, so that naturally shows up in my writing style. I come from a background where ministry leaders are elevated as "super spiritual" and they do not often communicate their own life's challenges or lessons they are learning from the Lord along the way. I feel everyone helps others when we live out loud, honestly and openly. I get that there are times when that may not be appropriate, as there are always exceptions to every rule.

The Bible says, "and they overcame him by the blood of the lamb and by the word of our testimony..." (Rev. 12:11). Therefore, I write this book as a testimony to all God has done, is doing, and will do in the future.

Though themes were repeated, and prayers sounded similar in some cases, I hope you enjoyed the book and I pray your faith was inspired to believe God for the impossible!

May you be blessed on your journey, and occupy your space in this world, with the time, treasure and talents he has entrusted you with, until He comes.

Bibliogrpahy

Chapter 5 Sources

1. Felitti, V. J., Anda, R. F., Nordenberg, D., Williamson, D. F., Spitz, A. M., Edwards, V., Koss, M. P., & Marks, J. S. (1998). "Relationship of childhood abuse and household dysfunction to many of the leading causes of death in adults." American Journal of Preventive Medicine, 14(4), 245-258.

2. Shonkoff, J. P., Garner, A. S., Siegel, B. S., et al. (2012). "The lifelong effects of early childhood adversity and toxic stress." Pediatrics, 129(1), e232-e246.

3. Chapman, D. P., Whitfield, C. L., Felitti, V. J., Dube, S. R., Edwards, V. J., & Anda, R. F. (2004). "Adverse childhood experiences and the risk of depressive disorders in adulthood." Journal of Affective Disorders, 82(2), 217-225.

4. Dube, S. R., Anda, R. F., Felitti, V. J., Chapman, D. P., Williamson, D. F., & Giles, W. H. (2003). "Childhood abuse, household dysfunction, and the risk of attempted suicide throughout the life span: Findings from the Adverse Childhood Experiences Study." JAMA, 286(24), 3089-3096.

5. Anda, R. F., Butchart, A., Felitti, V. J., & Brown, D. W. (2010). "Building

a framework for global surveillance of the public health implications of adverse childhood experiences." American Journal of Preventive Medicine, 39(1), 93-98.

6. Hughes, K., Bellis, M. A., Hardcastle, K. A., et al. (2017). "The effect of multiple adverse childhood experiences on health: a systematic review and meta-analysis." The Lancet Public Health, 2(8), e356-e366.

7. Bowlby, J. (1982). "Attachment and loss: Retrospect and prospect." American Journal of Orthopsychiatry, 52(4), 664-678.

8. Larkin, H., Shields, J. J., & Anda, R. F. (2012). "The health and social consequences of adverse childhood experiences (ACE) across the lifespan: An introduction to prevention and intervention in the community." Journal of Prevention & Intervention in the Community, 40(4), 263-270.

9. Merrick, M. T., Ford, D. C., Ports, K. A., & Guinn, A. S. (2018). "Prevalence of adverse childhood experiences from the 2011-2014 Behavioral Risk Factor Surveillance System in 23 states." JAMA Pediatrics, 172(11), 1038-1044.

10. Finkelhor, D., Shattuck, A., Turner, H. A., & Hamby, S. L. (2015). "A revised inventory of Adverse Childhood Experiences." Child Abuse & Neglect, 48, 13-21.

About the Author

Kathy J. Chastain is a lifelong resident of California and is a licensed marriage and family therapist in private practice, where she uses evidence-based theory and biblically based principles to help children, adolescents and adults work through their mental health and behavioral struggles. She has a deep conviction to use her voice to declare the word of the Lord and inspire faith in the hearts of those who read her words. She prays that you will trust God for the impossible in your life. She believes God is the God of the impossible and He will do what His word says He will do.

On Sale Now!

Please note: Kathy J. Looper has gone back to her maiden name Kathy J. Chastain

God can and will do the impossible. Will you answer the call?
There is a power working to crush families, silence churches, and shut down businesses. Yet, there is hope.
God is greater than any power that exists. He is all powerful. He has promised to go before us and make a way where there seems to be no way.

Redeem California is a strategic plan of action to call believers into actively participating in their faith, believing in God to show up and do the impossible, and identifying God-fearing people who can and will run for office in our cities, counties, state, and Congress. Now is the time. This is the hour. Will you answer the call?

**ON SALE NOW VIA AMAZON, BARNES&NOBLE,
AND OTHER MAJOR BOOK SELLERS.**